RAILWAY
BYLINES
Summer Special No.6

Railway Bylines Magazine.
Available the last Thursday of
every month. Price. £3.70

Editor
Martin Smith

All correspondence regarding editorial matters
should be addressed to;
RAILWAY BYLINES
P.O.BOX 1957, RADSTOCK, BATH BA3 5YJ
Tel: 01373-812048
(office hours only please)
Fax: 01373-813610
E-mail: smudger@ivycot49.freeserve.co.uk
Views expressed by contributors are not necessarily those of
the editor or publisher. Information is published in good faith,
but no liability can be accepted for loss or inconvenience
arising from error or omission.
The editor will be pleased to consider contributions
(articles, photographs or whatever) for publication but, while
every reasonable care will be taken, no responsibility can be
accepted for loss or damage, howsoever caused.
In the case of manuscripts submitted for publication, the
editor reserves the right to amend the text, if necessary, to suit
the style of the magazine. Where possible, edited/amended
texts will be returned to the contributor for his/her approval,
but the final decision rests with the editor.

The magazine **RAILWAY BYLINES** is
published monthly by Irwell Press Ltd.,
59a High Street, Clophill, Beds MK45 4BE. It
is printed in Luton by JetSpeed and
distributed by COMAG, London.
All distribution enquiries regarding the
NEWSTRADE and MODEL SHOPS should be
directed to Magazine Subscriptions, PO
Box 464, Berkhamsted, Herts HP4 2UR.
COPYRIGHT IRWELL PRESS ALL RIGHTS
RESERVED

Main cover photograph. Epping, 1957 – 67218 waits with the shuttle
train for Ongar. PHOTOGRAPH: THE TRANSPORT TREASURY

Upper cover photograph. Bromley - by - Bow Gas Works Peckett
0-4-0ST No.2, 4 April 1959. PHOTOGRAPH: JOHN R.BONSER

Title page photo. A Caley 0-4 -4T waits at Alyth, the terminus of the
ex-Caledonian branch in the eastern corner of Perthshire.
PHOTOGRAPH: ERIC ASHTON COLLECTION

Top right. If you want nooks and crannies you're reading the right
book. This is Folkestone Harbour, with the steeply-graded harbour
branch crossing from left to right at the end of the quay.
PHOTOGRAPH: GAVIN WHITELAW COLLECTION

Bottom right. Industrials? We do those, too. Here is Avonside
0-6-0ST ST.DUNSTAN at Snowdown Colliery, Kent, on 16
September 1964. PHOTOGRAPH: TOM HEAVYSIDE

Right. Picturesque branch lines R 'Us as well! 5592 leaves Mary
Tavy for Launceston in 1961. PHOTOGRAPH: PETER
BARNFIELD

Rear cover. The Cavan & Leitrim, March 1959. An Arigna-bound
train pauses at Cornabrone halt. Yes, this *was* a 'proper' stopping
place, though the only evidence of that was a name-board in the
hedge on the opposite side of the road. PHOTOGRAPH: DOUGLAS
ROBINSON

CONTENTS

Ambling through Mid Wales

Text and pictures by Peter Barnfield; picture captions by Bryan L. Wilson

During the Easter weekend of 1962 I was working as a volunteer on the Welshpool & Llanfair Light Railway. Having no transport of my own, I had managed to get a lift to Welshpool on the Friday but needed to make my own way home again on the Monday. This seemed an excellent chance to sample what was invariably known as the Mid Wales Line – the old Cambrian Railways line from Moat Lane through to its junction with the Brecon & Merthyr Railway at Talyllyn.

Trying to purchase a ticket for the Mid Wales Line the evening before was out of the question. The signalman/porter at Welshpool seemed quite unable to fathom out my intentions, even inviting me into the booking office to look through the massive Edmondson ticket rack just to prove that such a journey was impossible. In the end I settled for a single to Moat Lane, which he willingly dated before locking up the station and signal box for the night.

The following morning found me, after a hasty breakfast at the Boot Inn, standing on the platform in warm sunshine with 5 minutes to spare before the 8.55 to Newtown, Moat Lane and Aberystwyth. First to arrive however was a GWR Mogul with a train from Whitchurch; although the train terminated here it had a through coach for Aberystwyth. When 7819 HINTON MANOR arrived with three coaches from Shrewsbury, there followed som

Mid Wales tranquillity at Builth Wells. We are looking north, watching Ivatt Mogul 46519 head off into the distance with the 12.45pm 'all stations' to Moat Lane on 23 April (Easter Monday) 1962. Although the Mid Wales Railway started life as an independent concern and was taken over by the Cambrian, the imposing signal box we see here is pure GWR – it was brought into use in 1932 to replace the earlier 'North' and 'South' boxes. It boasted 39 levers. The local inspector, complete with the seemingly obligatory black mac over his arm, is walking back to the 'box. Champing at the bit to be the first over the level crossing is a typical example of road transport of the period – a Zephyr or Zodiac.

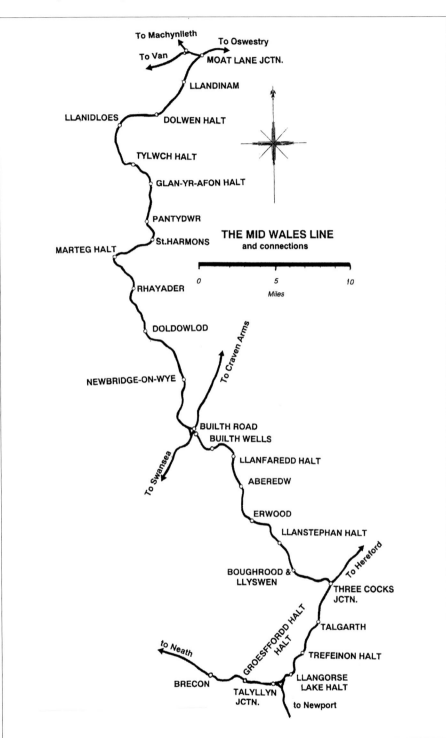

THE MID WALES LINE and connections

interesting shunting movements during which the Manor backed its train on to the through coach before we eventually set off about five minutes late.

We pottered along through rural Montgomeryshire, calling at all stations and crossing with 7802 BRADLEY MANOR at Newtown. There seemed to be far more staff than passengers at Moat Lane, where I alighted to find LM-type 2-6-0 46515 and two old GWR corridor coaches forming the Mid Wales train in

the other platform. After what felt like an age, BRADLEY MANOR ambled off towards Aberystwyth and the station returned to its slumbers. 46515 was blowing smoke over everything and the train guard reclined on a platform seat writing up his journal. Another LM Mogul that had been idling around rumbled off to the engine shed.

There was no blowing of whistles or waving of flags to announce our departure, but somewhere around 9.55 the guard

arose from his seat in the sunshine and ambled slowly towards his compartment, nodding as he did so in the general direction of the engine. So it was that the train quietly slipped away from the huddle of buildings that formed the railway community of Moat Lane and rattled along beside the River Severn, past Llandinam and Dolwen, lovely little wayside stations with passengers waiting for the guard to issue them tickets from the rack he carried, before we drew into

Having sneaked a look at life at Builth Wells, we now return to the start of the Mid Wales Line at Moat Lane Junction, a station which served no purpose for passengers other than for interchange. (Mid and North Wales had a few of these – for example, Dovey Junction and Bala Junction.) The name Moat Lane alluded to an old motte and bailey which can be seen in the distance on the right. Here we are looking east. The extremity of the Up 'main line' platform (though in this part of the world the term 'main line' was relative) is on the far left of the picture; this was an island platform. The Mid Wales Line leads off behind the signal box to the right of the Down main platform on which the photographer was

standing. The signal box is Moat Lane Junction East, a Dutton 'box of April 1890 with lapped boarding and decorative barge boards. By early GWR days it contained 53 levers. In the mid-distance on the left we see the fine pump house and water tank rearing up behind the Up starting signal. The tank and the rearward alignment of the boundary fence betray the fact that a loco turntable was once located here. This picture was taken during a return visit in August 1964 – i.e. a year and three-quarters after the Mid Wales Line and Moat Lane Junction had closed to passengers. The 'main' line through Moat Lane nevertheless remained open; it is still open today.

Llanidloes at about 10.15. Llanidloes was at one time the headquarters of the Mid Wales Railway Company and, befitting its once proud status, it was a rather imposing place with a vast two-storey brick and stone building of classic design, its huge bay window dominating the two platforms. The down side platform was an island; there were two signal boxes, a large goods shed, a two-road engine shed with a resident LMS Mogul, a long footbridge and an enormously wide road leading off down to the little town close by. At the time, there were about a dozen trains a day, including a number of short workings to and from Moat Lane, 7¾ miles away.

After crossing with another Mogul heading for Moat Lane, we were on our way again running beside the Afon Tylwch as the hills closed in about us, crossing and re-crossing the river as we plunged through a narrow tree-lined gorge. Riding with my head out of the window I could hear the roar of the rushing torrent even

above the clatter of the wheels. After Tylwch there were gently undulating meadows but the countryside became hilly again as we approached Rhayader where I found a really superb water column, the massive fluted pillar of which was topped by what looked like a gigantic Grecian urn.

Soon after Rhayader the line began to follow the course of the River Wye and actually ran along the Brecknock/Radnor border all the way to Three Cocks. At 11.22 we eased into Builth Road (Low Level) and I jumped out to explore the place while the train continued its 'all stations' journey to Brecon, 60 miles and 2½ hours away from Moat Lane.

Builth Road was a fascinating place to poke around, at least on a sunny day. The High Level station on the Swansea-Craven Arms line (the Central Wales Line) had some choice LNWR buildings and even a vintage lift in a wooden-clad slate roofed tower to exchange parcels between the two stations. Just down the

line from the station, with its fine view of the distant mountains, was a tiny single-road engine shed and Mogul 46519 skulking behind a row of coal wagons seemingly trying to elude my camera.

Back at the Low Level, I hastily terminated investigations of the refreshment room which appeared to be the preserve of a drunken farmer and his not particularly trustworthy looking dog and sought out someone to sell me a ticket. A knock on the ticket window and, yes – somebody eventually stirred within and I booked excess from Moat Lane and on to Bristol as easily as if this were an everyday occurrence. Or perhaps it was!

Just after midday 46505 came along with the completely empty 11.15 from Three Cocks. This train terminated at Builth Road and, while 46505 was running round, 46519 came off shed and set off down the line towards Builth Wells. 46505 then ran back into the down platform with its two coaches thus forming the 12.30 to Brecon. While all this

Table 185 — **MOAT LANE, LLANIDLOES, BUILTH ROAD, HEREFORD and BRECON**

WEEK DAYS ONLY

Miles	Station	am	am	am		am	am	am	am	am	am	pm	
	184Whitchurch dep		3 15										
	184Welshpool ,,		4 40								8 55		
	184Aberystwyth ,,										7 35		
—	Moat Lane Junction dep		5 45			8 30					9 55		
2	Llandinam		5 50			8 35					10 0		
5	Dolwen Halt		dd			8 41					10 6		
7¾	Llanidloes arr		6 2			8 45					1012		
	Llanidloes dep		6 5								1015		
11	Tylwch Halt		dd								1024		
12¼	Glan-yr-afon Halt										1029		
14¾	Pantydwr		6 24			Except Saturdays and School Holidays					1035		
16¼	St. Harmons		dd								1039		
19	Marteg Halt										1046		
21½	Rhayader		6 42								1054		
24¾	Doldowlod		6 50								11 1		
29	Newbridge-on-Wye F		6 58								11 9		
32½	Builth Road arr		7 6								1117		
	(Low Level) dep	6 30	7 7				9 10	9 56			1119		
34½	Builth Wells arr	6 33	7 10				9 13	10 0			1122		
	Builth Wells dep	6 35					9 30				1125		
36¼	Llanfaredd Halt						9 35				1129		
38½	Aberedw	6 44					9 39				1134		
41¼	Erwood	6 50					9 45				1140		
43½	Llanstephan Halt						9 51				1147		
45½	Boughrood and Llyswen	7 0					9 57				1152		
—	Mls Hereford dep								9 2				
—	5 Credenhill								9 13				
—	9¼ Moorhampton								9 22				
—	12½ Kinnersley								9 30				
—	14¼ Eardisley								9 36				
—	17½ Whitney-on-Wye								9 44				
—	21¼ Hay-on-Wye			7X55					9 54				
—	25¼ Glasbury-on-Wye			8X 2					10 2				
48¼	Three Cocks Junction arr	7 7		8X 7			10 4		10 8		1159		
	Three Cocks Junction dep	7 9		8 8					10 12		12 0		
50¼	Talgarth	7 16		8 14					10 17	From Newport (Table 121)	12 6	From Newport (Table 121)	
53	Trefeinon Halt	7 23		8 20					10 24		1213		
54¾	Llangorse Lake Halt	7 30		8 24					10 29		1218		
56	Talyllyn Junction arr	7 35		8 29					10 33		1223		
76	121Merthyr arr												
99¼	125Cardiff B ,,												
98¾	121Newport ,,	10 4									2 48		
96¾	121Cardiff D 131 ,,	9 47									3n28		
—	Talyllyn Junction dep	7 47		8 31					10 36	1046	1225	1 34	
58	Groesffordd Halt	7 52		8 35						1050	1230		
60	Brecon arr	7 57		8 41					10 44	1055	1235	1 42	

Miles	Station	pm	pm	am	pm	pm		pm	pm	pm	pm	pm	
	184Whitchurch dep			9 45								2 5	
	184Welshpool ,,			11 25		2 15						4 40	
	184Aberystwyth ,,			10 25		12 35			2 40			2 40	
—	Moat Lane Junction dep			12 27		2 55			4 45			5 27	
2	Llandinam			12 32		3 0			4 50			5 31	
5	Dolwen Halt			12 38		dd			4 56			5 37	
7¾	Llanidloes arr			12 44		3 10			5 2			5 45	
	Llanidloes dep					3 11						5 50	
11	Tylwch Halt					3 18						5 58	
12¼	Glan-yr-afon Halt					dd						6S 4	
14¾	Pantydwr					3 29						6 10	
16¼	St. Harmons					3 33						6 15	
19	Marteg Halt					dd							
21½	Rhayader					3 47						6 30	
24¾	Doldowlod					3 54						6 40	
29	Newbridge-on-Wye F					4 2						6 47	
32½	Builth Road arr					4 10						6 55	
	(Low Level) dep		1230			4 11						6 57	
34½	Builth Wells arr		1233			4 14					Saturdays only Commences 13th May, 1961	7 0	
	Builth Wells dep		1 20			4 18							
36¼	Llanfaredd Halt		1 25			dd							
38½	Aberedw		1 30		Except Saturdays and School Holidays	dd		Saturdays only					
41¼	Erwood		1 35			4 29							
43½	Llanstephan Halt		1 41			4 35							
45½	Boughrood and Llyswen		1 45			4 40							
—	Mls Hereford dep	1242								4 5			
—	5 Credenhill	1255								4 16			
—	9¼ Moorhampton	1 4								4 26			
—	12½ Kinnersley	1 12								4 34			
—	14¼ Eardisley	1 17								4 40			
—	17½ Whitney-on-Wye	1 24								4 48			
—	21¼ Hay-on-Wye	1 34								5 1			
—	25¼ Glasbury-on-Wye	1 43								5 9			
48¼	Three Cocks Junction arr	1 48	1 52			4 47				5 14			
	Three Cocks Junction dep		1 55		4 30	4 50				5 18			
50¼	Talgarth		2 1		4 38	4 56		From Newport (Table 121)		5P30	From Pontsticill (Table 121)		
53	Trefeinon Halt		dd		4 44	dd				dd			
54¾	Llangorse Lake Halt		dd		4 49	5 8				dd			
56	Talyllyn Junction arr		2 16		4 53	5 12				5P46			
76	121Merthyr arr									7T47			
99¼	125Cardiff B ,,									9S 2			
98¾	121Newport ,,		4 27							8S50			
96¾	121Cardiff D 131 ,,		5 6							8S49			
—	Talyllyn Junction dep		2 20		4 54	5 17		5 26		5P47	7 30		
58	Groesffordd Halt		2 25		4 58	dd		5 31		dd			
60	Brecon arr		2 30		5 4	5 25		5 36		5P56	7 38		

Miles	Station	pm	pm	pm		pm	pm	pm	pm	pm	
	184Whitchurch dep					4 10			6 50	6 50	
	184Welshpool ,,					7 15			3 45	1045	
	184Aberystwyth ,,					6 0					
—	Moat Lane Junction dep					8 3			9 26	1125	
2	Llandinam					8 8			9 31	1130	
5	Dolwen Halt					8 14			9 37	uu	
7¾	Llanidloes arr					8 20			9 42	1140	
	Llanidloes dep										
11	Tylwch Halt								Except Saturdays	Saturdays only	
12¼	Glan-yr-afon Halt										
14¾	Pantydwr										
16¼	St. Harmons			Saturdays only							
19	Marteg Halt										
21½	Rhayader										
24¾	Doldowlod										
29	Newbridge-on-Wye F										
32½	Builth Road arr										
	(Low Level) dep		7 55								
34½	Builth Wells arr	Except Saturdays	7 58					Saturdays only			
	Builth Wells dep			8 0							
36¼	Llanfaredd Halt			uu							
38½	Aberedw			uu							
41¼	Erwood			8 12							
43½	Llanstephan Halt			uu							
45½	Boughrood and Llyswen			8 20							
—	Mls Hereford dep	6 50						8 55			
—	5 Credenhill										
—	9¼ Moorhampton							9 15			
—	12½ Kinnersley	7 14						9 23			
—	14¼ Eardisley	7 19						9 31			
—	17½ Whitney-on-Wye	7 27						9 38			
—	21¼ Hay-on-Wye	7 39						9 50			
—	25¼ Glasbury-on-Wye	7 47						9 59			
48¼	Three Cocks Junction arr	7 53		8 24				10 4			
	Three Cocks Junction dep	7 54		8 25				10 5			
50¼	Talgarth	8 0		8 31			From Newport (Table 121)	1012			
53	Trefeinon Halt	8 7		uu				aa			
54¾	Llangorse Lake Halt	8 11		uu				aa			
56	Talyllyn Junction arr	8 15		8 43				1023			
76	121Merthyr arr										
99¼	125Cardiff B ,,										
98¾	121Newport ,,										
96¾	121Cardiff D 131 ,,										
—	Talyllyn Junction dep	8 16		8 45			9Z13	1025			
58	Groesffordd Halt	8 21		uu			uu				
60	Brecon arr	8 25		8 55			9Z22	1033			

aa Calls to take up on notice being given to the Station Master at Talgarth. Passengers wishing to alight must give notice to Guard at Talgarth
B Queen Street, via Merthyr
D Queen Street, via Bargoed
dd Calls if required on notice to Guard at previous *stopping* station or by giving hand-signal during daylight only
F 4½ miles to Llandrindod Wells Station
n On Saturdays arr 3 5 pm
P On Saturdays 4 minutes later
S Saturdays only
T Saturdays only and Second class only
uu Calls to set down on notice being given to Guard at previous *stopping* station
X Except Saturdays and School Holidays
Z On Saturdays 8 minutes later

Table 185—*continued* — **BRECON, HEREFORD, BUILTH ROAD, LLANIDLOES and MOAT LANE**

WEEK DAYS ONLY

Miles	Station	am	am	am		am	am	am	am	am	am		am
—	Brecon dep						6 50	7 35		8 15			1025
2	Groesffordd Halt							7 40		8 20			1030
4	Talyllyn Junction arr						6 59	7 45		8 25			1035
—	121Cardiff D 131 dep							To Newport (Table 121)					8 15
—	121Newport ,,												8 3
—	125Cardiff B ,,												7T36
—	121Merthyr ,,												9K28
—	Talyllyn Junction dep						7 0			8 30			1040
5¼	Llangorse Lake Halt						gg			8 33			1044
7	Trefeinon Halt						7 9			8 38			1050
9½	Talgarth						7 15			8 44			1055
11½	Three Cocks Junction arr						7 20			8 50			11 2
	Three Cocks Junction dep						7 22			8 51			11 6
—	13¼ Glasbury-on-Wye						7 26						11 8
—	17¼ Hay-on-Wye						7 36						1119
—	21 Whitney-on-Wye						7 44						1126
—	24¼ Eardisley						7 51						1136
—	26 Kinnersley						7 56						1141
—	29¼ Moorhampton						8 3						1148
—	32¼ Credenhill						bb						1155
—	38¼ Hereford arr						8 27						1216
14½	Boughrood and Llyswen									8 56			
16½	Llanstephan Halt									9 0			
18¾	Erwood									9 7			
21¼	Aberedw									dd			
23¼	Llanfaredd Halt									dd			
25¼	Builth Wells arr									9 22			
	Builth Wells dep					7 45			8 55	9 40			
27¼	Builth Road arr					7 49			8 58	9 44			
	(Low Level) dep					7 50							
31	Newbridge-on-Wye F					7 58							
35¼	Doldowlod					8 5							
38½	Rhayader					8 13							
41	Marteg Halt					8 20							
43¾	St. Harmons					8 29							
45¼	Pantydwr					8 32							
47¼	Glan-yr-afon Halt					8 39							
49	Tylwch Halt					8 43							
52½	Llanidloes arr					8 51							
	Llanidloes dep	6 30	7 10	8 5		8 55					11 0		
55	Dolwen Halt	6 35	7 15	8 10		9 1					11 5		
58	Llandinam	6 40	7 21	8 15		9 6					1110		
60	Moat Lane Junction arr	6 45	7 25	8 20		9 12					1115		
103½	184Aberystwyth arr					1135					[illegible]		
78½	184Welshpool ,,	7 20	8 8			9 55					12 0		
112½	184Whitchurch ,,	9 0				1212					2 40		

Miles	Station	am		pm	pm		pm	pm	pm	pm	pm		pm
—	Brecon dep			1210			1 20			2 5	4 10		5 5
2	Groesffordd Halt			1215			1 25			2 10	4 15		5 10
4	Talyllyn Junction arr			1220			1 30			2 15	4 20		5 15
—	121Cardiff D 131 dep			To Newport (Table 121)			10a58			To Newport (Table 121)			2S38
—	121Newport ,,						11a15						3S 0
—	125Cardiff B ,,												2S36
—	121Merthyr ,,												4S16
—	Talyllyn Junction dep						1 33				4 21		5C17
5¼	Llangorse Lake Halt						1 37				4 24		dd
7	Trefeinon Halt						1 42				4 30		dd
9½	Talgarth						1 48				4 36		5C32
11½	Three Cocks Junction arr						1 55				4 45		5C38
	Three Cocks Junction dep	1115					1 59	2 15			4 49		5 40
—	13¼ Glasbury-on-Wye							2 19			4 53		
—	17¼ Hay-on-Wye							2 29			5 2		
—	21 Whitney-on-Wye							2 37			5 11		
—	24¼ Eardisley							2 44			5 18		
—	26 Kinnersley							2 49			5 23		
—	29¼ Moorhampton							2 56					
—	32¼ Credenhill							3 6					
—	38¼ Hereford arr							3 21			5 59		
14½	Boughrood and Llyswen	1120					2 4				Except Saturdays		5 46
16½	Llanstephan Halt	1124					2 11						dd
18¾	Erwood	1140					2 17		Except Saturdays and School Holidays				5 57
21¼	Aberedw	1148					2 24						dd
23¼	Llanfaredd Halt	dd					2 28						
25¼	Builth Wells arr	1158					2 32						6 12
	Builth Wells dep	12 5			1245		2 40						6 16
27¼	Builth Road arr	12 9			1249		2 44						6 20
	(Low Level) dep				1250		2 48						6 22
31	Newbridge-on-Wye F				1258		2 55						6 30
35¼	Doldowlod				1 6		3 2						6 38
38½	Rhayader				1 15		3 10						6 48
41	Marteg Halt				1 21		dd						
43¾	St. Harmons				1 30		3 24						7 0
45¼	Pantydwr				1 33		3 30						7 4
47¼	Glan-yr-afon Halt				1 38		dd						
49	Tylwch Halt				1 42		3 40						7S16
52½	Llanidloes arr				1 50		3 48						7 21
	Llanidloes dep				1 54		3 50		4 15				7 25
55	Dolwen Halt				1 59		dd		4 19				dd
58	Llandinam				2 5		4 0		4 25				7 35
60	Moat Lane Junction arr				2 10		4 5		4 31				7 40
103½	184Aberystwyth arr				4 15		7 35		7 25				9 30
78½	184Welshpool ,,				2 55		[illegible]						8 35
112½	184Whitchurch ,,				4 46		7S51						10 8

Miles	Station	pm	pm	pm	pm		pm		pm		
—	Brecon dep	6 0	6 0		6 15		8 30		9 35		
2	Groesffordd Halt	6 4			6 20				9 41		
4	Talyllyn Junction arr	6 9	6 8		6 25		8 39		9 46		
—	121Cardiff D 131 dep				To Newport (Table 121)				6 55		
—	121Newport ,,								6 55		
—	125Cardiff B ,,										
—	121Merthyr ,,										
—	Talyllyn Junction dep	6 10	6 9				Saturdays only Commences 13th May, 1961		9 47		
5¼	Llangorse Lake Halt	6 14	6 14						9 53		
7	Trefeinon Halt		gg						9 59		
9½	Talgarth	6 23	6 23						1011		
11½	Three Cocks Junction arr	6 29	6 29						1016		
	Three Cocks Junction dep		6 30						1017		
—	13¼ Glasbury-on-Wye	Except Saturdays	6 34		Saturdays only				Saturdays only		
—	17¼ Hay-on-Wye		6 44								
—	21 Whitney-on-Wye		6 53								
—	24¼ Eardisley		7 1								
—	26 Kinnersley										
—	29¼ Moorhampton										
—	32¼ Credenhill										
—	38¼ Hereford arr		7 35								
14½	Boughrood and Llyswen		Saturdays only						1023		
16½	Llanstephan Halt								1028		
18¾	Erwood						To Bargoed (Table 121)		1036		
21¼	Aberedw								1042		
23¼	Llanfaredd Halt										
25¼	Builth Wells arr								1050		
	Builth Wells dep			7 40							
27¼	Builth Road arr			7 44							
	(Low Level) dep										
31	Newbridge-on-Wye F										
35¼	Doldowlod										
38½	Rhayader										
41	Marteg Halt										
43¾	St. Harmons										
45¼	Pantydwr										
47¼	Glan-yr-afon Halt										
49	Tylwch Halt										
52½	Llanidloes arr										
	Llanidloes dep										
55	Dolwen Halt										
58	Llandinam										
60	Moat Lane Junction arr										
103½	184Aberystwyth arr										
78½	184Welshpool ,,										
112½	184Whitchurch ,,										

a am
B Queen Street, via Merthyr
bb Calls to set down on notice to the Guard at Moorhampton and to take up on notice to the Station Master at Credenhill
C On Sats. dep Talyllyn Jn. 5 21 pm, Talgarth 5 34 and arr Three Cocks Jn. 5 39 pm
D Queen Street, via Bargoed
dd Calls if required on notice to Guard at previous *stopping* station or by giving hand signal during daylight only
F 4½ miles to Llandrindod Wells Station
gg Calls to take up for Glasbury-on-Wye and beyond on notice being given to Station Master at Talyllyn Junction
K Second class only
S Saturdays only
T Change at Pontypridd

Western Region public timetable, 12 September 1960 to 11 May 1961. This was a typical winter timetable of the period and was virtually identical to that which prevailed when photographer Peter Barnfield journeyed on the line in April 1962.

was happening about a dozen passengers had miraculously appeared. I found this somewhat surprising considering the remoteness of the place, but they came only to find that they were unable to board the train because all the doors were locked and the only chap with a carriage key had ambled off to the High Level station. One began to wonder if the doors had been locked all the way up from Three Cocks – it might explain the complete lack of passengers on the 11.15!

At 12.30 we heard the unmistakable hoot of an LMS engine from down the line, and Black Five 45145 hurried into the

About turn... Moat Lane Junction, this time looking west. This is one of the pictures taken by Peter Barnfield during his trip on the Mid Wales Line on 23 April 1962. The 8.20am Oswestry-Aberystwyth bears away to the right with 7819 HINTON MANOR at the head. On the left we have the 9.55 departure for Brecon. The shiny running in board invites us to change for Llanidloes, Rhyader, Builth Wells, Brecon and South Wales. Whereas many aspects of the Mid Wales Line – and, indeed, other lines in this part of the world – had an abundance of character, the same cannot be said for the concrete footbridge which looks well and truly out of place here. Among the station buildings at Moat Lane was a refreshment room. It was one of those places where two notes played on any instrument, or even just sung, could start an impromptu concert whilst awaiting a late connection.

High Level with five coaches from Swansea. Passengers and goods were transferred at a leisurely pace before we were off for Builth Wells, only three minutes away. Here we again found 46519 which had assembled the 12.45 to Moat Lane and departed in that direction soon after our arrival. The operating procedure for this long, straggling, lightly-used line with its several junctions and engine sheds was interesting and quite complex; it must have been a nightmare whenever something failed.

The 12.30 Builth Road-Brecon was just one of those complexities and was booked to spend from 12.33 to 1.20pm standing at Builth Wells while the engine crew sat on a station seat and ate their sandwiches. And why not indeed? So the entire complement of passengers did the same and there were eleven of us quietly munching away or nodding off in the noonday sun with all the carriage doors swung back open.

Our departure was delayed for some five minutes by the late arrival of a small Permanent Way inspection trolley, the open sort which has a flat, split windscreen in front of a seat on top of the engine and, if proceeding at anything more than a slow walking pace, threatens to break every bone in one's body. This machine came hurtling up the line and roared across the level crossing in a cloud

of exhaust, the driver handing the token to the signalman as the contraption ground to a halt.

We of course were unable to proceed without said token and, after the signalman had opened the gates to road traffic again, he found it impossible to cross the busy road to bring it to us. After what seemed like an age he eventually threw the token across the tops of the passing cars and our guard, more by luck than judgement, just managed to catch the thing, metal hoop and all, and take it to the waiting engine crew.

Under way once more we followed the Wye, threading through the trees along its banks, crossing and re-crossing this now wide river. Passengers, who had been quite numerous on the other sections of the line, were non-existent between here and Three Cocks, although as we came further south there were lots of sheep in the fields flanking the line. Many of these seemed to be almost magnetically attracted to that part of the Mid Wales line which was just in front of our locomotive. 46505, cylinder drain cocks open and whistle hooting frantically, failed to impress any sense of urgency on this ragged jumble of fleeces, which often ran for some way just in front of the buffers before diving through a gap in the fence.

At Three Cocks Junction I was able to witness the spectacle of three LMS

Moguls meeting with trains to and from Mid Wales and from Herefordshire, a fascinating sight at this rural station in the 'Y' of the lines from Builth Wells and Hereford and just over the Brecknock border. "Three Cocks change for Builth Wells, Llandrindod Wells, Llanidloes and the Cambrian Coast", proclaimed the huge sign on the old Hereford Hay & Brecon line's platform. How many holidaymakers bound for far away Pwllheli were heartened and excited by the sight of that running in board I wonder? I also wonder if the excitement hadn't worn a bit thin by the time they eventually saw the sea.

There was a long wait here as numerous passengers switched trains over the board crossings. We eventually pulled out well filled with people from the Hereford train, which had terminated here; its engine had already run round before we left – it would work home tender-first. The up Mid Wales train was hauled by 46515, which had brought me from Moat Lane that morning and had been turned at Brecon. The Hereford Hay & Brecon line was an outpost of the Midland Railway so I suppose it was appropriate to have this trio of ex-LMS engines meeting here; indeed, by the time of my journeys on these lines they seemed to work all the trains.

The straight alignment of the Mid Wales platform at Moat Lane clearly shows that that line was the first on the scene here. It was opened by the Llanidloes & Newtown Railway in September 1859; what eventually became the 'main line' to Machynlleth (and later Aberystwyth) did not open to passengers until January 1863. This is another 'post-closure' picture taken in August 1964. The Mid Wales Line had closed to passengers in December 1962 but ordinary freight traffic had been handled until May 1964. From 1964 until 1967 there was cement traffic for the Clywedog Dam project to the north-west of Llanidloes; the trains passed through and ran round here. There was also the occasional engineer's trolley. The platform buildings are remarkably large and substantial for a station which was merely an interchange point in the middle of nowhere. Substantial construction also extended to the concrete signal posts, but these were GWR additions – after the Grouping the GWR had had a blitz on replacing a number of former Cambrian signal posts (many of which had been in poor condition) by concrete posts.

The 9.55am to Brecon leaves Moat Lane behind. Centre stage is the engine shed; this is the 'rebuild' of 1957 which was in the 'Welsh' style – i.e. corrugated iron. The 'new' shed was constructed to the same dimensions as the previous building but with only a single pitched roof instead of double. The rebuild had a mere 5½ years railway life but still serves in private use. The public footpath to Caersws village runs alongside the shed from the station approach road.

The Midland Railway tentacles had reached no further than Three Cocks; the eight miles or so onwards from there via Talgarth to Talyllyn Junction were still Cambrian metals. Talyllyn Junction itself was on Brecon & Merthyr metals; here the sun cast long shadows across a 57XX pannier and the 2.5pm Brecon-Newport train. This was my train. Over

Llandinam station after closure to passengers. We are looking in the direction of Moat Lane. The parapets of the Afon Hafren (River Severn) viaduct can be seen a little beyond the level crossing. The road crossing the railway diverged from the A470 in the village of Llandinam (out of view to the right); after exiting scene left it meandered through the hamlets of Broneiron and Tyddyn. Returning to railway matters, Llandinam had a goods yard, perhaps because of the local presence of railway builder and coal mining entrepreneur David Davies whose mansion was nearby. The yard was latterly used as a storage point for pipes during the Clywedog Water scheme.

Right. We have reached Rhayader. Forget the station – what about this splendid water column formed of a fluted pillar topped by something resembling a Grecian urn. There were two such columns here – and that wasn't too unusual for this line as Mid Wales water columns generally had more than the usual quota of character. At the rear of the platform, the line between it and the goods shed served as an extra Up loop. This reflected the fact that Rhayader was a busy place with its livestock fairs, a corn mill nearby and cattle pens, granary and stables in the station area.

Below left. And now we come to the centre of the Mid Wales universe – Builth Road. In this case the Low Level station. The running in-board invites us to change for the Spa towns but, as if to suggest that the authorities were a bit stingy with the lettering (there were, after all, already a lot of letters on the running-in board), the 'etc' at the end is made up an '&' and a '£'. The station opened as Builth Road Junction in 1864 but was subsequently renamed Central Wales Junction even though it was never really a junction as such – the Central Wales Line passed overhead. The station was later renamed again, this time as Llechryd, and there was yet another renaming in 1889, this time as Builth Road. The 'Low Level' was added by BR in 1950. On the Down platform on the right, refreshment rooms had been opened by 1872 (and separate ones for First and Third class passengers); there was also the booking office, waiting room, 'Ladies' and the station master's office. Another item of interest – and a familiar sight to all visitors here – was the goods lift which took trolleys and parcels between the Low Level and High Level stations; it is the 'tower' to the right of the engine and train. Mere passengers had to climb the adjacent ramp. The Up platform on the left dates from 1893 when the crossing loop was provided. This picture was taken on 23 April 1962, the photographer having got off the 9.55 Moat Lane-Brecon in order to have a rummage around the two stations. By the time this picture was taken the only portions of the platforms in regular use were those with the white edging, but despite the less-than-intensively-used nature of things it appears that all was kept in a reasonable state of maintenance.

Builth Road Low Level on Easter Monday 1962 again, but this time looking from the High Level bridge as 46505 arrives with the 11.15 from Three Cocks. We have a better view of some of the facilities from this angle. Surely the 'Gents' is not that elaborate little building beyond the nameboard with the statutory fire buckets outside? Oh yes it is – 'gents' in the front portion of the building and the lamp room in the rear. And remember this is a place

where with two classes of refreshment room existed, so standards had to be kept up. The mounting block to reach the oil lamp can be seen in front of the Gents. A little to the right is a security pen which looks a more recent addition. But what was its use? Hazarding a wild guess, could it have been to provide safe keeping for the mails off the overnight York-Swansea Victoria train (which arrived at the High Level at 5.51am) until the GPO arrived to collect them

or until they could be taken on to stations on the southern part of the Mid Wales Line? As we said, that was only a guess; if anyone out there has more definite information please get in touch. (But before you ask – this is *not* one of our 'daft caption' competitions, so answers such as 'the security pen was for naughty sheep' will not get any sort of prize.)

We have enough time at Builth Road to look at that 'other' company – the LNWR. This is the High Level station on the Central Wales Line on 23 April 1962; the photographer is standing on the bridge over the Low Level line and we are looking towards Shrewsbury. The houses in the distance on the left (behind the Up platform) are in the appropriately named Railway Terrace. Farther into the distance is the goods shed.

yet another board crossing went passengers and luggage to be piled into three very crowded coaches.

In my compartment one corner was occupied by a huge fisherman, with all the gear, while in another was a chap who had only learnt of the line's existence from an old *Bradshaw's* and had come just for the ride. A party of girls was alighting at Pentir Rhiw in order to walk back to Talybont in time for tea, and the corridor was filled with three excitable boys with four even more excitable dogs who had been out rabbiting at Torpantau since dawn.

About two hours later, with people jamming the corridors like sardines, we arrived at Newport. I boarded a Cardiff-Portsmouth train for the run to Severn Tunnel Junction, had a short wait for the down Manchester, hauled by a King, and was walking down the incline at Bristol Temple Meads at 5.48pm, almost nine hours after leaving Welshpool.

In spite of late departures and what had seemed like awfully slow running, long pauses at stations and a very leisurely feel to operations, everything had more or less run to time and had connected where and when it should. Looking at the pace of life today I wonder how many people would now have the patience to endure such a journey when Welshpool, which seemed such a far away place to me in 1962, is now only three hours away from Bristol by car.

When the photographer returned to the area in August 1964 the Central Wales Line still served Builth Road High Level but the Mid Wales Line and the Low Level station had closed. This is the Up (Shrewsbury-bound) platform on the Central Wales Line. Although the running-in board has been shorn of its 'change for' suffixes, it still displays the name 'High Level'; that appendage was retained until 1969 despite the fact that it had been the *only* level since 1962! The platform building is rather attractive, with well-maintained barge boards and the date of 1884 on the end wall. The posters invite us to London and Cornwall – now there's a challenge from Builth Road! Then there's the Blue Pullman advert – these trains had already been in service for four years.

We are now a little beyond the south end of Builth Road High Level station. The ex-LNWR Central Wales Line is on the right and the station can be clearly seen in the distance. On the left is the curving loop to the Mid Wales Line; the additional sidings are for the exchange of traffic. The loop was regarded as part of the Central Wales Line, having been taken over by the LNWR in 1870. Builth Road North signal box (Low Level from 1935 when South 'box closed) can just be seen at the far end of the loop. It was another Dutton 'box, containing 38 levers. The single line in the middle of the frame is the permanent way department's siding. In an earlier picture caption we opined that Builth Road was never really a junction as such, but here we are showing the loop which connected the two lines. To explain... The loop offered through running between the Mid Wales Line north of the Low Level station and the Central Wales Line south of the High Level station, so without a reversal any through movement missed *both* stations. But all that was fairly hypothetical as, in practice, the loop was used mainly for exchanging wagons and was only very rarely traversed by through trains. In pre-Grouping days one of the very rare instances (possibly the only one?) of a passenger train using the loop was in July 1904 when the Royal Train travelled from Swansea (Victoria) to Rhayader for the ceremonial opening of the Elan Valley reservoir. Between the wars a summer Saturdays Barry-Llandrindod Wells service was routed via the loop, while during World War II a goods working from Crewe to Swansea and return was routed via Shrewsbury, Welshpool and Moat Lane and then used the loop to pick up the Central Wales Line.

At the southern extremity of Builth Road 'rail super centre' was the engine shed – or Motive Power Depot, to put it in official parlance. When photographed on 23 April 1962 Ivatt 2-6-0 46519 was in the yard. The timber-built single-road shed was ex-LNWR property but, by the time this picture was taken, the Central Wales Line was under Western Region jurisdiction and the shed was a sub to Shrewsbury (89A). Constructed in 1870, the shed was originally 100ft long but was shortened in 1941. There was once a shed at Builth Wells on the Mid Wales Line (sub to Brecon 89B) but it closed in September 1957 and the Oswestry and Brecon locomotives – such as 46519 seen here – were subsequently serviced at Builth Road. The strange thing about Mid Wales sub-sheds was that, although the line was flooded with Ivatt 2-6-0s from 1952 onwards, they were too long to turn on Llanidloes, Builth Road or Builth Wells turntables.

Returning to the Mid Wales Line, we move on to Builth Wells for a look at the local rush hour. The train on the left is the 12.45pm to Moat Lane which has 46519 out of view at the far end; the engine had come light from Builth Road shed. On the left is the water tank and on the right is the cast iron 'Gents' – no expense was spared on this line for comfort of travellers. On the right is 46505, still waiting with the 12.30pm Builth Road-Brecon. The engine was new to Oswestry in November 1952. At the beginning of 1963 the WR's Shrewsbury Division was incorporated in the LMR's Chester Division so 46505 became an LMR engine. Consequently, when it left Oswestry in April 1963 it remained on the LMR; it went initially to Willesden but later had stints at Chester, Birmingham and Manchester before going to Buxton in May 1967. It was withdrawn from there in June 1967, having gained fame as the last of the class.

As already mentioned the 12.30pm Builth Road-Brecon had a 47-minute wait at Builth Wells. A few more minutes didn't seem to matter on the Mid Wales, so the train waited for Permanent Way trolley A170W to roar in from the south. (Was there ever an *ABC* of these?) That fine water tank can be seen to advantage from this side.

46505 stands at Builth Wells in the Down platform with the 12.30pm from Builth Road to Brecon on 23 April 1962. This train had a 47-minute layover here. Strange as it might seem, that did make some sense as passengers on the 10.25am Central Wales Line train from Swansea Victoria had a good connection to Builth via Builth Road High and Low Levels; furthermore, connections with Hereford trains were later made at Three Cocks. In the late morning/ early afternoon passengers at Builth Wells could consider themselves well catered for – by Mid Wales standards, at least – as there were two trains to Brecon in the space of less than two hours. The line entering the yard to the right, in front of the Cambrian signal, leads to the turntable – one of those on which the Ivatts couldn't be turned! The goods shed is behind the signal and beyond that is the then-closed engine shed – another 'wiggly tin' building, albeit with 3ft brick walls at the base.

Builth Wells was not the only place in Mid Wales with a rush hour. This is Three Cocks Junction where, between 1.48pm and 1.55pm, three trains were due to arrive – a sort of 'Three at Three Cocks', if you like. By the early 1960s one could expect all three to be worked by the Ivatt Moguls. This was the scene on 23 April 1962. The train on the left is 46505 with the now-familiar 12.30pm Builth Road-Brecon. Beyond it is an unidentified member of the class running round – it had brought in the 12.42pm from Hereford and will return thence at 2.15pm. On the right, 46515 approaches with the 1.20pm Brecon-Moat Lane and is about to exchange tokens. This is train connections as they used to be!

The same seven-minute rush at Three Cocks, but on another day in 1962. This time, the Hereford train has just arrived with 46516 and a goodly compliment of passengers crosses to join the Builth Road-Brecon which is headed by 46507. The fireman rejoins his cab with the forward section token. On the far side we see the rear of the 1.20pm Brecon-Moat Lane in the Up Mid Wales platform. Three Cocks was another 'filling station' for passengers – the refreshment room sign can be seen on the gable end of the station building behind the signal box. The 'box, incidentally, is another example of Dutton's work; it opened in October 1890 and had a 40 lever frame.

Above. For southbound Mid Wales trains, the last four miles of the journey from Talyllyn Junction to Brecon were on former Brecon & Merthyr metals. When the photographer revisited Talyllyn Junction in the early summer of 1962 he found Collett 0-6-0 2240 waiting with a Brecon-Newport train; this was late in the day for 2240 as it was withdrawn in June 1962. A connecting service from the Mid Wales Line was at the opposite platform. Some rather nice signals completed the scene.

Middle right. Talyllyn Junction was another of those places where, five times a day, Up and Down trains connected to provide services between Mid Wales and Newport. The left-hand arm refers to the station's Up platform while the right-hand arm refers to the adjacent extension platform on the curve towards the north junction.

Bottom right. Yet another Mogul – this time it is 46516 looking rather smart – bides its time at Talyllyn Junction extension platform in 1962 while waiting for the connecting service from Newport. Although the main part of the station dated from 1869 this platform was not added until the mid-1890s, its purpose being to enable two Newport services to cross and still make a Mid Wales connection.

LITTLE AND LARGE — Take One
Photographs from The Transport Treasury

A 4-6-0 tank engine might sound like a comparatively hefty beast, but there were some such engines which were far from hefty. The pair seen here were certainly at the small end of the scale. Built by the Baldwin Locomotive Company of Pennsylvania for military use in Europe during World War I, they were two of six which were purchased second-hand from the WD by the 2ft-gauge Ashover Light Railway. All six were named after the children of the company chairman, General Thomas Hughes Jackson, but it remains unknown whether that name theme was adopted out of nepotism or as a boast about the gentleman's fertility. These pictures were taken at Clay Cross & Egstow station yard in May 1937 by

which time the Ashover was a 'goods only' line, its passenger services having ceased in 1936 after only 11½ years of operation. As noted in the NGRS's book *Over Here* (reviewed in the May edition of *Bylines*), the fortuitous fact that the Ashover had a batch of identical locomotives meant that they could be cannibalised for parts and, by using this tactic, HUMMY was kept going until 1946 and PEGGY until July 1949. We concede that these locomotives might not have been the most sleek or modern-looking machines in the world, but who needs beauty when you've got as much gritty character as this?

LITTLE AND LARGE – Take Two
Photographs by J.T.Rutherford; The Transport Treasury

Most industrial railways were lightly constructed and many had sharp curves and, as these factors placed restrictions on the size, weight and wheelbase of the locomotives used, it is little wonder that the humble 0-4-0T or 0-6-0T came to be the archetypal industrial locomotive. So who would have thought that comparatively large tender engines had any place on industrial systems? To prove that there was no such thing as an unbreakable rule, the 0-4-2 above is CALDER No.5 which spent all its life at William Dixon's Calder Ironworks near Airdrie. We can tell you that it was built by Dübs & Co of Glasgow in 1873, but

that's the sum total of our knowledge. To our embarrassment, we do not know exactly why Dixon's used tender engines (over the years they had six), but we imagine that it was something to do with there being a reasonably lengthy journey between the company's collieries and the ironworks. Do we hear the sound of a 'Dear Editor' letter? In an attempt to redeem ourselves we *can* tell you a little bit more about Harton Coal Company No.5, seen in the picture below. Built by the North Eastern Railway in 1881 (for book purposes, at least, it was allegedly an NER rebuild of an 0-6-0 of 1856), it was purchased by

the Harton Coal Co in 1929 and used on the South Shields, Marsden & Whitburn Colliery Railway on the north Durham coast (see *Railway Bylines 1:1*). The SSMWCR was over three miles in length and ran, not only coal trains, but also passenger trains, so there was a point to using tender engines. Ironically, though, of the company's various 0-6-0s (over the years it had sixteen different examples, albeit not simultaneously), No.5 was used mainly for shunting at Whitburn Colliery.

NARROW GAUGE IN THE MED
the Cyprus Government Railway
Photographs by Hugh Ballantyne

The CGR's tiny one-off 0-6-0T No.1 was built by the Hunslet Engine Company in 1904. It was the maker's No.846 and was shipped to Cyprus in parts for assembly there. With 2ft wheels, 8in x 12in cylinders and a 160lb boiler, it weighed 10 tons 15 cwt and had a nominal tractive effort of 3,584lbs. It was used during the construction of the railway but, in later years when it was required to undertake 'ordinary' work, its lack of power meant that the only work for which it was suitable was between Famagusta station and the harbour. This is where it was photographed on 10 November 1951 – it is seen bringing two bogie opens (the

engine's maximum loading!) loaded with oil drums up to Famagusta station. By this time No.1's livery was black with red rods. The bogie wagons, incidentally, were known as the 'EHS' type; the initials stood for 'Egyptian High Sided', the wagons having been acquired from Egypt during the Great War. After the closure of the CGR on 31 December 1951, No.1 was earmarked for preservation. However, that was not altogether straightforward as the locomotive had been included in the deal which had been made with the scrap merchants who were contracted to dismantle the railway. To make good the deficit, No.1's new all-steel boiler

(which had been fitted as recently as 1948) was replaced by the original one and the new boiler was offered up to the scrap dealers with the balance being made up by an equivalent weight of scrap rails. So No.1 was saved. It was placed on static display outside what had been Famagusta station. In 1972 it was restored to its original livery and some mechanical restoration was also undertaken, but it was not possible to restore it to full working order. Even if mechanical restoration *had* been possible, there was nowhere on the island for it to operate.

The island of Cyprus in the eastern Mediterranean only ever had one 'main' railway line and a short branch line, and even that modest set-up didn't last for very long. Built to the gauge of 2ft 6in, the railway in question – the Cyprus Government Railway – extended for 76 miles from Famagusta via Nicosia to Evrykhou. The solitary branch line was a smidgin less than a mile in length from Famagusta station to the harbour. The harbour branch was brought into use in late 1904 to assist the contractors engaged on the construction of the harbour itself. The Famagusta-Nicosia section of the railway opened for business in October 1905 and the line was extended to Morphou in March 1907; it finally

reached Evrykhou (1,300ft above sea level) in June 1915. Evrykhou was a small, remote village so the decision to terminate the line there might seem somewhat bizarre, but there were thoughts that Evrykhou could become a staging post for tourist traffic to the Troodos Mountains.

For a while the railway did reasonably well from goods and mineral traffic, but the level of passenger traffic failed to excite. During the 1920s road transport began to compete for the modest amount of traffic that was on offer, and this started an irreversible decline in the railway's already unspectacular fortunes. The line west of Nicosia to Evrykhou was closed as early as 1932, but the section between

Nicosia and Kalokhorio reopened to freight traffic the following year.

The system was heavily used during the war, but this proved to be a mixed blessing as, by 1945, the whole system was worn out, especially the track which was a very lightweight 30lb/yd. Any thoughts of major renewal work were tempered by the fact that, in 1941, a new main road between Famagusta and Nicosia had been completed, and road transport now offered serious competition for the little peace-time traffic that was on offer. The railway struggled on for a few years but it came as little surprise when, in 1951, closure was announced. There were various protests against the proposed closure, but the authorities had

The CGR's principal engine shed and workshops were at Famagusta. This was the scene on 5 March 1952 – about nine weeks after the closure of the railway and just before the scrap dealers moved in. The engines on view are our old chum No.1, 2-6-0 No.22 (Nasmyth Wilson W/No.710 of 1904) and 4-4-0 No.12 (Nasmyth Wilson W/No.708 of 1904). On the right is railcar No.4.

The CGR had four outside-framed Kitson 4-8-4Ts. They had 2ft 6in coupled wheels, 13in x 18in cylinders, 160lb boilers, nominal tractive effort of 14,600lb and weighed in at 36 tons 5 cwt. Two of the four were purchased in 1915 for £2,846 each and the other two came in 1920 for £8,160 each. The similarity between these engines and the famous Kitson-built Barsi Light Railway 4-8-4Ts and the Leek & Manifold Railway's shorter 2-6-4Ts is obvious. Here we see No.44 and No.42 at Famagusta shed. The CGR only ever had twelve steam locomotives, so the numbering system which used separate sequences for different types of locomotives – hence a 'No.44' – was perhaps a little extravagant. Back to the nitty-gritty... When this picture was taken the two engines has been positioned for inspection by officials from the Sierra Leone Railway with a view to purchase. But that did not happen and both engines were scrapped.

their way and the last public trains ran on 31 December of that year. There were however still the occasional steamings for other purposes, as one or two of our photographs confirm.

Fortunately for all of us today, seventeen-year-old photographer Hugh Ballantyne went to live in Cyprus in November 1951 – just before the railway closed – so he was able to record the scene during the last month or so.

(Most of the information for these notes and captions has been shamelessly taken from The Story of the Cyprus Government Railway *by B.S.Turner, published by Mechanical Engineering Publications in 1979.)*

No.44 was the last engine to be built for the CGR – as Kitson W/No.5298 it arrived on the island in 1920. Here it stands in the afternoon sunshine outside Famagusta shed on 7 November 1951. The photographer recorded its livery as red, albeit very faded, with black buffer beams. Features to note include the single central buffer, the copper-capped chimney, the cow-catcher, the huge headlamp, the remarkably spacious cab and the balance weights on the ends of the axles instead of on the wheels themselves. Given that Cyprus was a British colony, it was unsurprising that all the locomotives and passenger stock and much of the goods stock and other railway equipment used on the island were supplied by British companies.

Although the CGR closed to public traffic at the end of 1951, one or two duties lingered on. This picture was taken on 24 October 1952 – i.e. almost ten months after the railway's 'closure' – and shows 4-4-0 No.11 (Nasmyth Wilson W/No.707 of 1904) standing at the quayside at Famagusta Harbour with one of the water-tank wagons. The hose has been run out from the 700-gallon tank to supply fresh water to the harbour tug *Desdemona*. Alongside the engine are lifted rails; most of the recovered railway material was exported to Italy as scrap in March and April 1953.

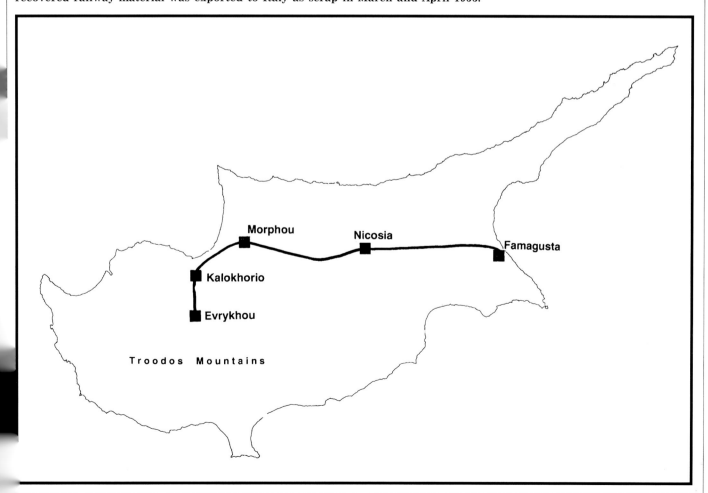

CGR 2-6-2T No.31 comes up the 1 in 44 grade from the harbour towards Famagusta station on 7 November 1951. The engine was built by Nasmyth Wilson in 1907 (W/No.799); it had 2ft 3½in coupled wheels, 10in x 15in cylinders, a 175lb boiler, weighed 20 tons 2 cwt and had a nominal tractive effort of 7,160lbs. The engine's livery is very faded red with black buffer beams. In the distance on the left are the walls of the old Turkish city. Our trusty guide book tells us that these walls have an average height of 50ft and are 27ft thick in some places.

he delightful 'colonial'-looking Nasmyth Wilson 2-6-0 No.22 (which we saw earlier on shed at Famagusta) percolates
utside Nicosia shed on 13 November 1951. The engine was painted black with dark green lining and red buffer beams.
o.22's vital statistics were: 2ft 3½in coupled wheels, 10in x 15in cylinders, 175lb boiler, weight 14 tons 3 cwt (plus the
iminutive tender), tractive effort 7,160lbs. Like most of the CGR engines No.22 was eventually converted to oil-firing, as
onfirmed by the oil drum on the tender. Fuel – or, rather, the lack of it – had always been a problem for the railway as the
sland of Cyprus had no coal. The alternatives were to import coal – usually from Britain – or to burn wood. The option of
ood burning came to an end during World War II when timber supplies ceased, and as the supply of coal from Britain was
nderstandably erratic at that time, a short-term solution was to import some coal from South Africa. The long-term
olution to the problem was to convert the locomotives to oil-burning, the programme commencing in 1944. No.22's conversion
as undertaken in 1945.

nother alternative to coal- or wood-burning was internal combustion. A total of six internal combustion railcars was
urchased between 1932 and 1941, though to be precise it was six *chassis* which were purchased. They were all built by the
ell-known firm of D.Wickham & Co of Ware, Hertfordshire, and had Ford engines. The bodies were made and fitted on the
sland. This specimen is 'Railcar G' which had a 12-seat body and was powered by a 4-cylinder engine with the drive by
eans of a conventional prop shaft. Behind it is a locally-built 16-seat trailer. The ensemble is seen running into Famagusta
tation from the cutting and tunnel with the 7.30am from Nicosia on 26 November 1951. One conspicuous aspect of this
icture is the very lightweight 30lb/yd permanent way.

Top left. The railcars were accommodated at the carriage sheds at Famagusta. These sheds were completely separate from the steam shed and workshops, and this helped to keep the railcars and carriages well away from the soot and grime. From left to right we have: First/Second composite coach No.3 and Third Class No.11 (both built by the Metropolitan Railway & Carriage Co in 1905), 25hp chain-driven 'Railcar C' (which was, in fact a large inspection car – it was supplied by the Drewry Car Co but is thought to have been built by Baguley Cars of Burton on Trent) and railcar 'V8-1' (locally-built body on a 1940 Wickham chassis powered by a Ford V8 engine). This picture was taken on 28 November 1951.

Above. And it's back to steam... And how! This wonderful spectacle is 2-6-0 No.21 (Nasmyth Wilson W/No.709 of 1904) clattering over the lightweight 30lb/yd track near Trakhoni, seven miles from Nicosia, with the 6.10am daily steam service from Famagusta to Nicosia on 7 December 1951. The train is formed of a pair of Metropolitan Railway Carriage & Wagon vehicles – a Third Class and a Second Class brake compo. In the distance on the left are the Kyrenia Mountains which, incidentally, have two peaks of over 3,000ft.

Left. Having made occasional reference to the CGR's less-than-spectacular level of passenger traffic – especially as the years progressed – this packed-to-the-rafters 12-coach train might seem a tad contradictory. But don't be deceived. We are looking at a troop train. And it's not just any old troop train – it is the very last troop train to run in Cyprus. It was used to convey men of the Bedfordshire & Hertfordshire Regiment from Famagusta to Nicosia on 12 November 1951 and was photographed about a mile out of Famagusta. The engine is No.43, one of the CGR's last two 'Barsi-lookalike' Kitson 4-8-4Ts which were purchased in 1920. Digressing totally... for those who might be tempted to visit Cyprus to look for remains of the railway, may we recommend *Cyprus Phrase Book no.95* – a 'three-way' Anglo-Greek-Turkish phrase book. (We kid you not – we have a copy of this very booklet in our possession!) The booklet was presumably written in the days when Cyprus's railway was still operating as it gives rail travellers translations of such invaluable phrases as: 'You can be joyful and regulate the temperature of the sedan with this lever', 'Make fast, sir, the train is not balancing', 'Where is the defective luggage examined?' and our particular favourite 'Excuse me, sir, I would accompany you very joyfully but unfortunately some imperious circumstances are impeding me'. (To prove that we are not making all this up, the Turkish for the last phrase is: 'Mazur görünüz bay, memnuniyetle size refakat etmek isterdimse de, maalesef bir takim mübrem ahval bana mani oluyorlar'. So there!) Elsewhere in the book are translations of such phrases as 'I ought to have some small change because I mind to visit the exposition', 'You have become all pale; I have ate the quails', 'Make fast and sharpen the razor after soaping my visage' and 'Barber – you have beheaded my pimple'. (Honest!)

WIGAN REVISITED
Notes by Bryan L.Wilson

It seems as if the level crossings on the Springs Branch in Wigan were irresistible to photographers. We featured some superb period views of Manchester Road Crossing and Belle Green Lane Crossing in *Bylines 6:1* (December 2000) and – would you believe it? – four more pictures of the very same crossings turned up just as we were finishing work on this *Summer Special*. Once again we found ourselves looking at fascinating 1950s street scenes. How could we possibly resist them? The two pictures on this page show Manchester Road Crossing as it was on 26 July 1956. The upper picture looks towards Wigan town centre. The signal box from which the crossing was operated is just out of frame to the right. Note the LNWR automatic gate stop in the roadway; this was raised by the gate drive rod mechanism as the gate approached it, thus avoiding a 'stop' sticking up in the roadway and presenting a hazard, especially for cyclists. The lower picture is of the other side of the crossing – we are still looking towards town. The stops holding the gates in position can be seen, as can one of the wicket gates for pedestrians. 'Gleem' might seem a little inappropriate but one must say that the houses look well maintained and – have you noticed – there is no litter.

t is still 26 July 1956, and now we move farther up the branch to Belle Green Lane Crossing. In the upper picture we are
ooking north-east with the controlling 'box (if there were anything operational left to control, that is) on the left. The
ower picture is an about turn – we are looking in a south-westerly direction. Looking at the crossing, a more disreputable-
ooking example of railway infrastructure would be hard to find. The road surface in the upper picture isn't anything to
vrite home about either – the stone setts have been patched with tar or asphalt and this has made a bad surface even worse.
'he undergrowth behind the gates proves that weeds are not a Railtrack invention; at the time these pictures were taken
he line was still open (formal closure did not come until April 1958), but it is clear that the 'still open' status was theoretical
s all traffic had obviously ceased. Ironically, despite the Board of Trade's 'minimum standards' requirements which
tated that single gates were preferable to double ones at level crossings, the crossings seen here – and, indeed, the majority
hroughout the country – had double gates as this kept the length of each gate to a minimum and thereby gave more
trength. The use of galvanised tie rods on each side of each gate (as seen in all four of our pictures – attached to the gate
n the pictures opposite but to the post in the pictures on this page) provided even more strength and rigidity. At least, this
vas the theory.

DESFORD COLLIERY
by Mike Kinder

The rural location of Desford Colliery is clearly visible in this general view. The village of Desford is a good two miles away to the left of the photo; Bagworth is much nearer – a mere half-mile to the right. The recently built washery and screens are in the foreground. The line to the right is the wagon tippler road; the building is the tippler itself. The bridge-like structure crossing the lines behind carried the waste for the spoil bank – this picture was actually taken from half-way up the spoil bank! In this latest reconstruction of the colliery the number of lines under the screens has been reduced and the growing road transport and the facilities for it are clearly evident. The houses along the road in the distance were built for colliery officials and deputies. All were demolished owing to subsidence when the colliery closed. PHOTOGRAPH: COURTESY M.CONIBEAR

Desford Colliery was the last to be opened in the North-west Leicestershire Coalfield. It lay about eight miles to the west of the city of Leicester on the coalfield's southernmost edge. An attempt had been made by the Lindridge Coal Company to sink a shaft about a mile north of Desford village in 1875. However, this venture, headed by a Mr.Shore, the owner of Lindsay Hall, encountered difficulties in the form of the Thringstone Fault and, despite two further sinkings (one in 1883 and the other in 1887) and the production of a little coal, the project had to be abandoned when the money ran out. A further attempt to reach coal was made in 1900 by a Mr.Edward Bramall, this time about a mile further to the north-west, nearer to Bagworth. Mr.Bramall achieved the success that had eluded Mr.Shore and, with Charles Moody in charge of engineering operations, two shafts were sunk to the Lower Main seam – a depth of about 238 yards. These two shafts eventually gave access to eleven coal seams. The shafts were operated independently, each being used by men and coal; No.1 shaft served the lower seams and No.2 the upper, an arrangement which continued until 1957. While the shafts were being sunk and before screens were built, any coal that was raised was dumped in the yard. Local legend has it that John Thornley, who kept a farm at Bagworth, took the first load away with his horse and cart. The 'proper'

raising of coal at Desford eventually started in 1902, the concern trading under the title of the Desford Coal Company.

The internal railway
In 1901 a single track was laid from the Midland Railway's Leicester-Burton line to the colliery. Desford Colliery Sidings signal box was opened on the up side on 7 July of the same year. On 9 September 1901 the still-unfinished colliery took delivery of its first locomotive, an inside-cylindered Hudswell Clarke 0-6-0ST (W/ No.579), which was used to bring in materials and equipment for the development of the colliery. It was named COUNTESS OF WARWICK in acknowledgement of the Countess's ownership of the land on which the colliery was sited.

It was not until 1908 that sufficient coal was coming out to require the use of a second locomotive; the newcomer was Peckett 'C' class 0-6-0ST W/No.1175, which was christened DESFORD. The two locomotives remained in charge of all internal railway working until 1927 when a third locomotive was acquired, the owners of the colliery presumably having optimistic expectations at the end of the General Strike. The new arrival was another Peckett 'C' class 0-6-0ST (W/ No.1733); it was named DESFORD No.2. (Interestingly, Peckett built only eight of their 'C' class engines and four of them worked in the Leicestershire Coalfield.)

With the arrival of DESFORD No.2 the fleet of three locomotives was to prove adequate until after World War II.

The growth and production of the colliery continued apace, and the Ordnance Survey map of 1930 reveals that a fairly substantial rail system had developed. There were extensive sidings on the west side of the LMS main line with trailing junctions to both up and down sides. One of the sidings stretched well over a quarter of a mile to the road bridge at Merrylees. From these sidings a double track diverged towards the colliery, and after about 150 yards it fanned out into seven exchange sidings, logically known as Desford Colliery Sidings. This is where LMS/BR working ended. The exchange sidings extended for some 200 yards before converging to become double track again. Almost immediately these again fanned out, this time into fourteen loop lines, nine of which served the screens. The other five loop lines passed around the north side of the screens and, at the west end of the colliery, converged with the other lines to form a headshunt. Over the eighty or so years of the colliery's existence the track layout underwent various modifications to meet changing circumstances and demands.

The usual working practice at the time was for a colliery locomotive to bring empties from the exchange sidings and haul them into the headshunt. It then propelled them into the required screen

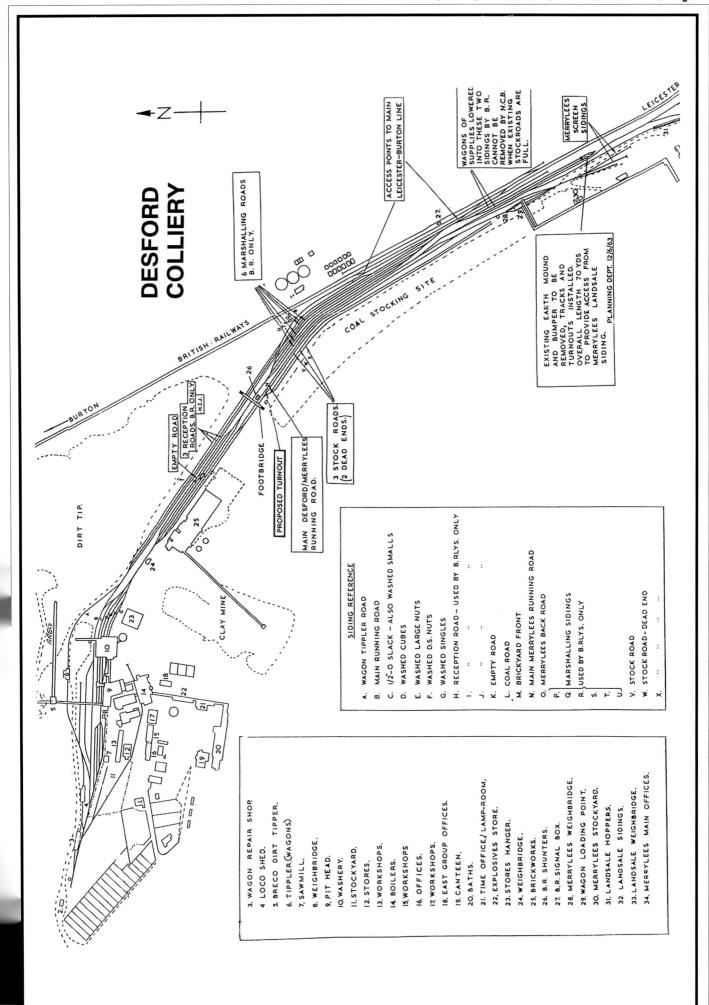

DESFORD COLLIERY

6 MARSHALLING ROADS
B. R. ONLY.

ACCESS POINTS TO MAIN
LEICESTER–BURTON LINE

WAGONS OF
SUPPLIES LOWERED
INTO THESE TWO
SIDINGS BY B.R.
CANNOT BE
REMOVED BY N.C.B.
WHEN EXISTING
STOCKROADS ARE
FULL.

MERRYLEES
SCREEN
SIDINGS

LEICESTER

BRITISH RAILWAYS

BURTON

COAL STOCKING SITE

EMPTY ROAD

3 RECEPTION
ROADS. B.R. ONLY.

FOOTBRIDGE

PROPOSED TURNOUT

MAIN DESFORD/MERRYLEES
RUNNING ROAD.

3 STOCK ROADS.
(2 DEAD ENDS.)

DIRT TIP.

CLAY MINE

EXISTING EARTH MOUND
AND BUMPER TO BE
REMOVED, TRACKS AND
TURNOUTS INSTALLED.
OVERALL LENGTH 70 YDS
TO PROVIDE ACCESS FROM
MERRYLEES LANDSALE
SIDING.   PLANNING DEPT. 12/6/63

SIDING REFERENCE

A. WAGON TIPPLER ROAD
B. MAIN RUNNING ROAD
C. 1/1½–0 SLACK – ALSO WASHED SMALLS
D. WASHED CUBES
E. WASHED LARGE NUTS
F. WASHED D.S. NUTS
G. WASHED SINGLES
H. RECEPTION ROAD – USED BY B.RLYS. ONLY
I.   :   :   :
J.   :   :   :
K. EMPTY ROAD
L. COAL ROAD
M. BRICKYARD FRONT
N. MAIN MERRYLEES RUNNING ROAD
O. MERRYLEES BACK ROAD
P.   :   :   :
Q. MARSHALLING SIDINGS
R. USED BY B.RLYS. ONLY
S.   :   :   :
T.   :   :   :
U.   :   :   :
V. STOCK ROAD
W. STOCK ROAD – DEAD END
X.   :   :   :

3. WAGON REPAIR SHOP.
4. LOCO SHED.
5. BRECO DIRT TIPPER.
6. TIPPLER (WAGONS).
7. SAWMILL.
8. WEIGHBRIDGE.
9. PIT HEAD.
10. WASHERY.
11. STOCKYARD.
12. STORES.
13. WORKSHOPS.
14. BOILERS.
15. WORKSHOPS.
16. OFFICES.
17. WORKSHOPS.
18. EAST GROUP OFFICES.
19. CANTEEN.
20. BATHS.
21. TIME OFFICE / LAMP-ROOM.
22. EXPLOSIVES STORE.
23. STORES HANGER.
24. WEIGHBRIDGE.
25. BRICKWORKS.
26. B.R. SHUNTERS.
27. B.R. SIGNAL BOX.
28. MERRYLEES WEIGHBRIDGE.
29. WAGON LOADING POINT.
30. MERRYLEES STOCKYARD.
31. LANDSALE HOPPERS.
32. LANDSALE SIDINGS.
33. LANDSALE WEIGHBRIDGE.
34. MERRYLEES MAIN OFFICES.

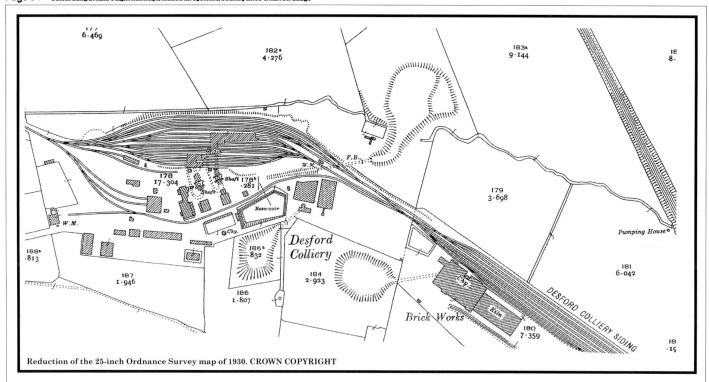

Reduction of the 25-inch Ordnance Survey map of 1930. CROWN COPYRIGHT

roads where they were filled with the appropriate coal sizes – singles, doubles, cubes, house coal, slack.

Another feature of the 1930 Ordnance Survey map is a brick works alongside the exchange sidings. These works had been opened in 1927 by a subsidiary company, the Desford Brick Company Ltd, and as can be seen on the OS map they had their own siding. The brick works are still operational today as part of the Hanson empire.

Developments
In the early 1930s the Desford Coal Co implemented a major reconstruction programme at the colliery. This entailed an extensive rearrangement of the colliery layout and the installation of much new plant, including new winding engines and screening plant and conveyor belts to take the coal off the faces. Another aspect of the work was the replacement of the original wooden head gear with six-legged concrete structures. In addition, the Upper Main seam coalfaces were mechanised, 30 and 40hp Mavor & Coulson 'Samson'

cutting machines being installed. The improvements at the colliery seem to imply that the Desford Coal Company had great confidence in the long-term future of the pit, despite the inauspicious nature of the prevailing circumstances. Following the General Strike – during which the colliery had closed for 26 weeks – the workforce had been only on part time; this situation prevailed for most of the Depression period (except during the worst parts of the winters) and continued until the beginning of World War II. It was only then that Desford went back into

A view of the washery and screens from the same side but from ground level. Note the quite impressive quality of the track. The Hunslet Austerity awaits action on the right. On the left is one of the colliery's weighbridge offices. PHOTOGRAPH COURTESY M.CONIBEAR

The shafts have just been sunk at Desford and the workers are posing for the camera. Note the original wooden headgear. PHOTOGRAPH: COURTESY M.CONIBEAR

continuous full time production. During the lean years, incidentally, a buzzer used to sound at the pit to inform the workforce that there was no work the next day. One of the ex-miners recounted how his father sometimes had to go to work for nothing – 'on the mim' – in order to be able to go to work the next day.

There were further developments at the colliery in 1939/40. These included the construction by Davenport Engineering Co of a new ferro-concrete cooling tower (the smallest to be built at a colliery at that time) to replace the old wooden one, the reconstruction of the boiler plant and extensions to the screens. Another aspect of the development was a new landsale

depot at the southern end of the site (in the Merrylees area, more of which anon). The depot included a line of concrete bunkers which were raised on concrete legs and fed with coal from above by wagons which had been propelled on to the top of the structure by a locomotive; the coal was dropped into lorries below by means of door operating levers.

As a result of the flooding of the early Lindridge shaft, fear of a similar fate meant that Desford saw little development to the south. However, on the strength of borehole evidence that there was a considerable quantity of workable coal to the south, the decision was taken to drive, quite separately, two drift mines

to obviate any possibility of flooding the Desford workings. These drifts, approximately 710 and 750 yards long, were driven in 1942 and became the Merrylees Drift Mine. The first coal was brought out in 1943 and was taken to Desford for washing.

In 1946 a fourth locomotive arrived at Desford. It was a five-year-old Bagnall 0-4-0ST (the only four-coupled steamer ever to work at Desford) which had previously worked at Royal Ordnance Factory No.10 at Rearsby, between Leicester and Melton Mowbray. The little Bagnall was acquired principally to work the coal and waste from the recently opened Merrylees Drift Mine to the preparation plant and spoil bank respectively at Desford. However, this task proved too exacting for it and in 1948 it was despatched to Ellistown Colliery, a few miles to the north-west. It had been intended to name this locomotive MERRYLEES but, although this name was later used in NCB files, it was never applied to the locomotive.

The boiler house
An integral part of the colliery was the boiler house. It accommodated nine Lancashire boilers which provided the power for the winding gear, hot water and the heating for the baths, the canteen and fitting shops etc, and also the electricity for the two rows of houses where the colliery officials and deputies lived, along the road just outside the colliery. From *circa* 1950, however, the boilers had one less role to fulfil when the National Grid took over the supply of electricity to the colliery houses.

A post-steam view of Desford Colliery signal box and spoil bank, looking in a north-westerly direction on 16 April 1970. The siding behind the 'box was traditionally used for Wellingborough bound traffic and perhaps this was still the case. The line between here and Knighton South Junction was singled eight months after this picture was taken, the last two 'boxes on the Leicester side closing at the same time. Desford 'box survived the closure of the colliery by well over two years – it did not close until 29 June 1986 when Leicester power box came into use, at which point the line was singled on to Bardon Hill. By then, the 'boxes on the Leicester side had all long since closed. PHOTOGRAPH: M.A.KING

A view towards the colliery from the exchange sidings on 2 March 1978. Hopper wagons and the block train merry-go-round system are now the order of the day. The three lines on the right are the reception lines for empties from BR. The two lines on the extreme left had at one time served Merrylees, but by this time they seem to have served as stock storage roads. On the left is the brickworks – which is still operating on a large scale – and on the right is the spoil bank. PHOTOGRAPH: KEVIN LANE

State ownership

Britain's coal industry was nationalised on 1 January 1947 and Desford Colliery duly became part of the NCB's East Midlands Division. One of the very few incidents occurred in 1948 when an explosion in No.1 pit injured 14 men. It could, of course, have been much, much worse. Prior to the explosion Desford had been a naked light pit, but this accident led to the use of safety lamps – and not only at Desford but throughout the Leicestershire coalfield. This incident apart, despite the very dangerous nature of the mining industry Desford had a comparatively trouble-free existence.

During the post-war and early NCB period the colliery worked from 6am to 10pm and the enginemen operated two shifts – 6am-2pm and 2pm-10pm – with two or three engines in steam. Horace Yorke was the engine fitter (though he did some driving as well) and was well known for his skills and general expertise. He was succeeded by Lindsay Eaton whose father had been the enginewright in pre-NCB days. The men were also responsible for lighting up and preparing, a process which started at 5am. As soon as the engines began work at 6am their first task was shunting the screens, after which a steady succession of wagon rakes was run by grav-

ity down to the weighbridge – movements were controlled by a couple of wagon lowerers – and then into the exchange sidings for collection by a main line engine.

The other daily duties included taking coal to the boilers and running waste up the spoil bank. Ten wagons was the normal number propelled up to the embankment along which the spoil was distributed, though trains could be formed of up to twelve wagons if the conditions were considered sufficiently propitious; for twelve-wagon trains, two engines normally had to be used. (It must have been a wonderful spectacle. Was nobody ever there to record it on film?) Inclement

DESFORD COLLIERY – summary of standard gauge locomotives (listed in order of acquisition)
Summary of makers: EE – English Electric; **HC** – Hudswell Clarke; **HE** – Hunslet Engine Co; **HL** – Hawthorn Leslie; **P** – Peckett & Sons; **RH** – Ruston & Hornsby; **S** – Sentinel (Shrewsbury) Ltd; **WB** – W.G.Bagnall

No. and/or Name	Type	Maker; W/no.	Cyls./h.p.	Wheels	Built	Acquired	Disposal
(COUNTESS OF WARWICK)	0-6-0ST	HC 579	13" x 20" (i)	3' 3"	1901	New	12.1957 scrapped
DESFORD	0-6-0ST	P 1175	14" x 20" (i)	3' 2"	1908	New	6.1967 to Cashmores (scrap)
DESFORD No.2	0-6-0ST	P 1733	14" x 20" (i)	3' 2"	1927	New	8.1966 scrapped
-	0-4-0ST	WB 2651	14½" x 22" (o)	3' 6½"	1941	1946 ex-ROF Rearsby	1948 to Ellistown Cll'y
DESFORD No.3	0-6-0ST	HE 3170	18" x 26" (i)	4' 3"	1944	7.1947 ex-Moor Green Cll'y	1966 to Nailstone Cll'y
-	0-6-0ST	P 1118	14" x 20" (o)	3' 7"	1907	1951 ex-Nailstone Cll'y	10.1965 scrapped
-	4w VBT	S 9398	6¾" x 9" (v)	2' 6"	1950	1952 Thos.Hill demo	1952 returned to Thos.Hill
-	4w VBT	S 9538	6¾" x 9" (v)	2' 6"	1952	1952 Thos.Hill demo	1952 returned to Thos.Hill
-	4w VBT	S 9544	6¾" x 9" (v)	2' 6"	1952	1957 ex-Ellistown Cll'y	1958 to Nailstone Cll'y
-	0-6-0DM	RH 347747	333hp	3' 11"	1957	New	1973 to Newdigate Cll'y
SOUTH LEICESTER No.1	0-6-0ST	P 1587	16" x 22" (o)	3' 10"	1924	6.1965 ex-South Leics Cll'y	1966 to Nailstone Cll'y
* PHOENIX No.2	0-6-0ST	HL 2611	14" x 22" (o)	3' 6"	1905	1967 ex-Donisthorpe Cll'y	8.1968 to Cashmores (scrap)
15/2/13	0-6-0DH	HE 6288	260hp	3' 4"	1966	New	9.1974 to Cadley Hill Cll'y
15/2/12	0-6-0DH	HE 6289	260hp	3' 4"	1966	New	4.1983 to Snibston Cll'y
15/2/14	0-6-0DH	HE 6692	260hp	3' 4"	1967	6.1968 ex-Whitwick Cll'y	5.1969 to Newdigate Cll'y
15/3/3	0-4-0DE	RH 420139	165hp	3' 2½"	1958	5.1970 ex-Ellistown Cll'y	7.1970 to Ellistown Cll'y
-	0-6-0DH	HE 6693	260hp	3' 4"	1967	7.1970 ex-Newdigate Cll'y	7.1984 to Snibston Cll'y
-	0-6-0DH	RR 10212	455hp		1964	3.1971 ex-Measham Cll'y	6.1972 to Nailstone Cll'y
NCB 20	0-6-0DH	EE D1200	380hp		1967	6.1972 ex-Nailstone Cll'y	8.1975 to Rawdon Cll'y
15/2/17	0-4-0DH	RH 544875	287hp	3' 6"	1968	11.1975 ex-Donisthorpe Cl'y	8.1984 to F.Berry (for scrap)

* *PHOENIX No.2:* The presence of this loco at Desford has not been confirmed
There is a school of thought that two other Ruston & Hornsby diesels might have served briefly at Desford (see text)
COUNTESS OF WARWICK – name not carried in later years

Wagons

In pre-NCB days the Desford Coal Company wagons were painted black with the name Desford in white. At about the time of Nationalisation Desford is recorded as having contributed to the Railway Clearing House pool a total of 579 'main line' wagons:

- 1 x 6-ton
- 6 x 8-ton
- 522 x 10-ton
- 50 x 12-ton.

There were also 98 internal user wagons:

- 73 x 8-ton
- 15 x 9-ton hoppered
- 2 x 15-ton hoppered
- 3 x 17-ton hoppered
- 5 x 20-ton hoppered

Of those, the 9-ton type (at least) was used to tip coal for the boilers.

By September 1963 the internal wagons comprised:

- 12 side-tipping steel wagons (used for boiler slack)
- 50 low-side wooden wagons, capacity 6-7 tons
- 111 high-side wooden wagons, capacity 10-12 tons.

Merrylees had:

- 54 steel wagons, capacity 21 tons
- 20 steel hoppers, capacity 15 tons
- 25 high side wooden wagons, capacity 10-12 tons

weather could quickly defeat their efforts and it would be back to the bottom, drop off two or three wagons and start again.

The first trip was always fairly early so that the six men employed at the tip could start shovelling the spoil out of the wagons – a task made all the more difficult by the large quantity of stone, often of quite massive proportions, in it. (A bulldozer went in during the hours of darkness to push the spoil away from the track). The writer was given a vivid description of the hardships involved, particularly in the winter months – and it doesn't need much imagination to visualise conditions at the top of a pit bank in mid-winter. To make their lot marginally more acceptable, the men knocked together a wooden hut to provide some shelter and relief; one much needed home comfort was a stove of quite massive proportions which has been built for them by one of the fitters. The men at the tip were not necessarily the only ones to suffer. At busy times, if there were any trainees on the site, half a dozen of these would suddenly find themselves conscripted into participating to obtain some 'valuable experience'!

It should be added that other methods were also employed for conveying the waste to the spoil bank. Slurry from the washery went up on a conveyor belt, and by 1957 an aerial ropeway had been installed. This was the Breco system – it was *not* the familiar highly-elevated pylon variety but was a compact steel structure which had buckets hanging on it and ran up the side of the spoil bank. This system was rather more efficient than the old rail-operated system; furthermore, by this time the height of the pit bank had presumably compelled recognition of the dangers involved in rail operation. This continued in use until some time in the mid-1960s, at which stage loading shovels and dumpers took over.

More locomotives

To go back to the start of the NCB era in 1947, the nation's collieries were required to make considerable increases in production to combat the severe coal shortages throughout the country. At Desford, another locomotive had to be brought in to deal with the additional workload. This engine was a much-travelled Hunslet 'Austerity' 0-6-0ST (W/ No.3170 of 1944) which, as WD 75120, had been sent new to Longmoor in March 1944. In November of that year it had been sent to France but had been stored at Calais until January 1947, when it had returned to England. Six months later it was to be found at Moor Green Colliery in Nottinghamshire. (The NCB was acquiring large numbers of ex-WD 'Austerities', and the Moor Green Colliery railway was being used as a holding point for them as they returned from the continent.) WD75120 stayed at Moor Green for only a month before being despatched to Desford Colliery where it became DESFORD No.3, the name being painted on the sides of its tanks. However, it lost its name at some fairly early stage (possibly during a very lengthy visit in 1955/56 to the Area Workshops at Bath Road, Moira), after which it spent the remainder of its life in anonymity.

In the early 1950s a £1,000,000 reconstruction scheme was implemented at Desford. Extensive alterations were made to No.1 Pit top, shaft and bottom to enable four-ton minecars to replace the small tubs which had been previously used. Coal winding was then concentrated on No.1 shaft, with new main roads being driven. Mechanisation of the coal cutting was greatly extended over this period as a result of new technology and, in 1958, a new washery and screens were installed and the sidings remodelled accordingly.

Partly due to the reconstruction work and partly as a consequence of the opening of Merrylees Drift Mine, the total production at Desford rocketed from 609,293 tons in 1947 to an all-time record of 1,064,674 tons in 1954. During this period of rapidly increasing production a

...view the other way along the exchange sidings to the main line and the sidings there. (The photographer was standing on a footbridge that spanned the whole system). The signal box is visible behind the far end of the rake of slack loaded hopper wagons. The four lines to the left of the wagons, the line on which they are standing and the line to the right formed a block of six marshalling sidings which were for BR use. PHOTOGRAPH: KEVIN LANE

Main line workings

The LMS and BR Working Timetables for 1935, 1956/57 and 1968/69 reflect the development and subsequently the decline of the colliery. In 1935, in the up direction, trains went out to:
• Peterborough, 9.35am
• Wellingborough, 10.05am
• Humberstone Road, Leicester, 9.05pm
There were also trip workings to Knighton South Junction, West Bridge and 'Generator' (Leicester Electricity Generating Station).
In the down direction there were trains to Mantle Lane, Coalville, at 4.05pm, 6.20pm and 10.05pm.
   In 1956/57 activity was fully representative of the large outputs being achieved at that time .
In the up direction trains left for:
• Northampton, 4.47am
• Peterborough, 5.08am
• Wellingborough, 7.10am
• Wellingborough, 4.59pm
There were also the trip workings to Knighton South Junction, West Bridge and Leicester Electricity Generating Station.
   By 1968/69 the WTTs indicated an inexplicable lack of activity. Although the output at the colliery was now on the decline the annual total for 1968 was still 857,984 tons (670,000 tons in 1969), yet the WTT lists only a single departure – to Wellingborough at 8.20pm. The only other disturbance to the tranquillity was the arrival of empties from Hams Hall at 9.59pm. On the other hand, a working railwayman recalls that most of the coal in the 1960s and 1970s went to Mantle Lane for remarshalling and forwarding to Drakelow, Birchills, Nechells and Hams Hall power stations, with all of the coal, in the last four years of production, going out in the Leicester direction for Rugeley and Didcot power stations. He also clearly recalls the awkward manoeuvres needed to get the train properly formed when leaving in the Coalville direction – and even more clearly what a terrible job it could be to get the train on the move on a rising grade from a dead start.

sixth locomotive arrived at the colliery. This was an elderly Peckett 'B2' class 0-6-0ST (the outside-cylinder equivalent of the 'C' class) which had been delivered new to nearby Nailstone Colliery in 1907; it had remained at Nailstone until its transfer to Desford in 1951. Although the Peckett had been named PHOENIX No.3 during its days at Nailstone, there is no indication that it carried a name while at Desford.

In 1952 two other steam locomotives arrived at Desford. They were standard vertical-boilered Sentinels – one was rated at 100hp and the other at 200hp –

but their appearance at Desford was only for demonstration by Thos.Hill, the well-known dealers and agents. It would seem that the authorities at Desford were fairly unimpressed with the Sentinels as they were soon returned to Hill's. Nevertheless, in 1957 a third Sentinel – a 200hp example – was transferred to Desford from Ellistown Colliery; it remained at Desford only until 1958 when it was transferred to Nailstone Colliery. It is possible that this Sentinel was a temporary replacement for Desford's veteran Hudswell Clarke 0-6-0ST COUNTESS OF WARWICK – the

colliery's very first locomotive – which was scrapped on site in December 1957.

Engine sheds and shops
There seem to have been three different engine sheds at the colliery over the 80-plus years of its life. The first one, which can be seen on the accompanying 1930 Ordnance Survey map, was a single-road dead-end shed, on the south west side of the screens. This was replaced in 1933 by a shed on the north-west side of the site; this was a single-road through shed which held two engines and had an inspection pit.

In 1958 another new engine shed (dead-end, like the original) was built just beyond the 1933 shed but, even though the track was laid and smoke vents were fitted, for reasons unknown it was never used for its intended purpose. (An NCB document of 1963 refers to the building as a wagon repair shop, not an engine shed, but it was never used for that either.) Instead, it was used to store various equipment and, more importantly, for work on the hydraulic chocks which had been invented by Matthew Smith, the under-manager at Desford. The chocks were used to support the roof of coal seams. Their invention won Smith fame throughout the mining world in the 1950s and they became the foundation for the modern roof support systems used on every mechanical coal face in the world. The work undertaken in the 'engine shed' at Desford entailed either coupling the hydraulic pipes to chocks and generally preparing them (after their arrival from the manufacturers and prior to their journey underground) or undertaking any subsequent repairs that became necessary. This work was originally done

Desford's first engine, Hudswell Clarke W/No.579, stands outside the shed on 28 August 1954. It had at one time been named COUNTESS OF WARWICK but there is no sign of the name here. The colliery clearly had a very substantial water tank though how the water was actually conveyed to the locomotive is not so clear! **PHOTOGRAPH: JOHN R.BONSER**

Five years earlier, on 21 August 1949, the anonymous COUNTESS OF WARWICK was photographed shunting the stock yard. An ex-collieryman who started work at Desford in 1946 clearly remembers seeing the engine with its brass nameplate, so that seems to narrow down the date when anonymity was adopted. The concrete structures that replaced the original wooden head gear are quite conspicuous, as is the boiler-house chimney. The wagon to the left of the loco, lettered D B C, is one of the Desford Brick Company wagons which regularly found themselves on internal use here or taking slack to the brick works boilers. Visible everywhere are numerous pit props and also split bars which were used for wall supports underground. PHOTOGRAPH: F.A.WYCHERLEY COLLECTION

outside, irrespective of the weather conditions, but when it became clear that the new engine shed was not going to fulfil its intended function, pressure was applied by Tom Boulton, who was in charge of the hydraulic equipment and was also responsible for visiting and dealing with the various manufacturers such as Dowty, Gullick and Dobson, and permission was granted to move in.

There was also a small wagon shop with a staff of three, who were mainly responsible for the maintenance and repair of the internal wagons (approximately 100 in number) which were used for such purposes as taking coal to the boilers and spoil to the spoil tip. In addition to the wagon shop (which disappeared at the end of the 1950s as a result of the reconstruction, after which the wagons were repaired outside), there was a tub shop where the underground coal tubs were given any necessary repairs.

The men
From the mid-1940s Jim Johnson was in charge of the loco side, and among the drivers (of both steam and diesel) were Joe Massey, Arthur Adcock, Les Bott and Len Spencer. The first three of those gentlemen would also assume the roles of fireman and shunter as required. Les Spencer was excused the additional duties as, being a little older, he was granted the privilege of sticking to driving.

By the late 1950s the manpower at the shed comprised a foreman, seven engine drivers, eight shunters and two loco

cleaners/firers (nights only). The foreman also served as fitter, spending most of his time in the shed. Each engine was manned by a driver and shunter on all shifts. There was also a shunter responsible for shunting all the wagons into the screen shunting bays on each shift and four wagon lowerers, two working at the screens and two from the screens, running the wagons down to the weighbridge on a brakestick and then on to the BR sidings.

Quite unusually for a colliery railway, the track was kept in a generally good state of repair, maintenance being carried out on a daily basis. Arthur Hurd, who was killed one foggy morning, hit by a raft of moving wagons on their way from the screens to the exchange sidings, was the foreman of the platelayers/linesmen, among whom were Jack Moon, Albert Gough and a Mr.Platts. The good condition of the track meant that derailments and accidents were very few and far between; those that did occur were usually unrelated to track problems – as in the unfortunate case of Arthur Hurd. There were quite a few examples of damaged limbs while shunting was in progress under the screens, but the men spoken to could not recall anything involving an engine or train derailment.

Despite these eulogies about the good condition of the permanent way and the consequent lack of derailments, it should be emphasised that it was a rather different matter at the spoil bank. Keeping the track there in good condition was, of course, simply impossible and over the years derailments were quite

numerous as the engines stormed up 100 yards or so of precipitous bank with their loads. However, Jim Johnson, with three or four men and the skill gained from long experience, was adept at returning wagons (or occasionally an engine) to the track, using only wooden blocks and an engine to haul the offending items back on – no easy task when the operation was taking place half way up the bank! And even a little reflection on these spoil heap activities makes it clear how lucky the men were to escape a disaster at some point. The compiler vividly remembers visiting Mountain Ash on one of the days that some wagons of waste were propelled on to the tip, which was of comparatively modest steepness and size. The engine accelerated along the normal out-of-alignment colliery track to gain sufficient momentum on the approach to the bank; this was alarming enough, but the sight and sound of the engine, working flat out through the facing points and up an apparently trackless and grey, oozing quagmire of a bank, were of volcanic and quite terrifying proportions. Retrospective contemplation of the psychological effects of such activity on the modern day Health and Safety person, though, is manna to the soul!

Diesel dawn
The first diesel came to Desford in 1957. It was a Ruston & Hornsby 333hp 0-6-0 diesel-mechanical W/No.347747, one of only nine in the maker's 'LWS' class. (Interestingly, Ruston turned it out with the wrong works number –337747 – and

Peckett 0-6-0ST DESFORD in action on 2 May 1963. Former Desford railwaymen remember her as 'a lovely engine' from which the Colliery got its full money's worth. PHOTOGRAPH: R.C.RILEY; THE TRANSPORT TREASURY

had to track it down and change the numberplate!) It had a Paxman 8RPH engine driving through a large mechanical gearbox – an attempt to find a cheaper alternative to the expensive electric transmissions used in most large diesel shunters at that time. Its designated duty was the haulage of Merrylees coal to Desford, a task it performed quite efficiently until this work came to an end in 1966. Shortly after this, however, its performance deteriorated rapidly and, despite having several costly repairs in the 1970s, it remained notoriously unreliable for the rest of its existence. The machine left Desford for Newdigate Colliery on 25 April 1973, and the state it was in when it reached Newdigate would

A fine portrait of DESFORD, this time standing alongside the engine shed which, by this time, had been re-roofed. In the background is the unnamed Peckett W/No.1118. It is standing outside the building which, according to some, was intended to be a new engine shed but, whether or not, it was never used as such. PHOTOGRAPH: R.C.RILEY; THE TRANSPORT TREASURY

suggest that Desford had been only too thankful to be rid of it. Perhaps remarkably, it survives in preservation at the Rutland Railway Museum.

Working the system
During the late 1950s and the first half of the 1960s the usual procedure was for the Austerity to shunt empties from the reception sidings to Desford screens, to undertake general shunting at the colliery itself, and to collect any incoming supplies. One of the Pecketts acted as landsale loco, shunting landsale 'fulls' from Desford Sidings to Merrylees landsale sidings and empties from Merrylees to Desford; it also shunted Desford house coal and Merrylees house coal and spoil to the Merrylees Hoppers (and usually 'fulls' to Desford boiler house). The Ruston diesel was used to take empties to Merrylees and unscreened coal from Merrylees to the tippler house at Desford during the 6.00am-2.00pm shift, and Merrylees unscreened coal and Desford spoil to the Desford tippler during the 2.00pm-10.00pm shift.

The layout of the sidings at the colliery was altered in 1958 when a new washery and screens were installed.

Underground
Other forms of motive power employed at Desford warrant a mention, in particular the underground types. Firstly the animal variety. In the early 1950s there were up to 16 ponies working underground; they were used exclusively for taking materials and equipment to the coal faces. There were also two or three on the surface, their task being to pull tubs of stone from the washery to a small secondary spoil bank near the new pit-head baths. (In the early 1950s the blacksmith's shop was still one of the largest in the colliery.) There was also a horse and cart which performed odd jobs round the yard, such as carrying materials and equipment to wherever they were needed. The last pit pony was retired in 1963; it had latterly been used to pull tubs of stone from the screens to a tipper to be taken up the main bank.

In the post-war period various systems of transport operated underground, many of them simultaneously. After the massive mechanisation programme of the 1950s had been implemented, all the coal was brought to the bottom of No.1 shaft by a series of conveyor belts which increased in width from 24" to 42" as they picked up more coal at each junction. (Those at the faces travelled at about

3mph whereas the main trunk belts which went to the bottom of the shafts travelled at about 15mph.) Prior to that, endless rope systems had brought tubs of coal from the conveyor belt systems along the main roadways to both pit bottoms.

Another innovation of the period was the introduction, *circa* 1958, of 'manriding' trains to convey the miners to and from the coal faces. The first such trains comprised open cars which ran on 2ft gauge tracks and were operated by endless rope haulage. The track ran for about ¾-mile from the bottom of No.2 shaft (there were improvised platforms at each end) and served the various districts. Tubs could be attached to front or rear, as required, to carry equipment and materials. The 'guard' had a wooden rod with a metal contact strip at the end (usually a power hacksaw blade, the teeth ensuring a good contact!) to short across two wires running along the roof, by which means he could signal to the driver of the electric motor which operated the endless cable when he wanted to stop, start or change direction.

In the 1970s 'high speed' manriders, manufactured by N.B.Wild & Co, were installed, the new cars being enclosed for protection. (There were about eight 'carriages' to a train – a sort of Desford District Line!). These could travel at 10-12mph as opposed to the 4mph of the earlier cars. The higher speed necessitated the abandonment of the earlier signalling system and the adoption of radio signalling with a leaker feeder system that was pioneered at Desford. Over the years further enclosed cars, their superstructure made variously of metal or fibre glass, were provided by different

On shed on 11 July 1963 was one of the other Peckett's – the nameless and numberless W/No.1118. Note the spark arrester.
PHOTOGRAPH: HORACE GAMBLE

A fine study of SOUTH LEICESTER No.1 – though there is no evidence of the name here – in action at the back of the siding alongside the main line on 26 June 1965. The engine must be working Merrylees trains as those were the only workings tha took Desford Colliery locos down past the exchange sidings. The engine had only very recently arrived from South Leiceste Colliery to help out. PHOTOGRAPH: IVO PETERS

manufacturers. By the end of the 1960s, following test trials in a nearby field(!) the Becorit trapped rail system was also installed, operating beyond the system just described and delivering men, equipment and materials to the new and greatly extended coal faces. Transfer systems in the form of overhead cranes were provided to enable a switch of the equipment and materials, loaded on pallets, from one system to the other. Becorit 25hp and 40hp diesel locomotives, running on patent synthetic tyres which had a terrible tendency to wear out with great rapidity (though the state of the track was at least partly responsible), operated on a ground mounted mono-rail. It was one of the first installations of its kind in Britain. The 25hp locomotives had Perkins 3-cylinder engines with Hunslet flame-proofing whereas the 40hp ones had German 4-cylinder engines and Ronyon flame-proofing.

Later came some 50hp locomotives which, apart from their power rating, were virtually the same as the 40hp type. This loco system operated exclusively in the main roadways of the 'Antwerp' district of the mine workings. (In pre-NCB days the various parts of the workings were usually referred to by nicknames instead of numbers and these nicknames were usually perpetuated by the men in NCB days). The Becorit trapped rail system was also installed elsewhere in the workings, but in these other sections the trains were powered not by locomotives but by endless rope haulage.

One other underground locomotive must be mentioned. This was a

Greenwood & Batley flameproofed four-wheeled battery-operated machine which had a 17.5hp motor on each axle and a driver's cab with a full set of controls at each end. This ran on a 2ft gauge track and operated exclusively in the 'Fourteens' district of the colliery workings, being used to carry men and equipment. It arrived in August 1968. Interestingly, a bit of creative accounting was involved in its arrival at Desford. Capital allocated to Baddesley Colliery was used to buy it but, when the auditors found out, they insisted that the machine be moved to Baddesley and then transferred back to Desford. It remained at Desford until 1976 when it went to Swadlincote.

More steam

But to return to the surface… At one point in the mid-1960s Desford was having serious motive power problems. As noted earlier there was a daily requirement for two steam locomotives and the Ruston diesel, but in early 1965 the Austerity was taken out of service for repair, Peckett 1118 was struggling along with a cylinder moving independently of the frames (it was put out of its misery by being cut up in October 1965), and Peckett 1733 (which had left Desford for Nailstone Colliery in September 1960 but had returned to Desford in late 1961 or early 1962) was in very poor condition – 'a mechanical wreck', as one former NCB man put it. The only other engine in good condition was DESFORD, even though its boiler was time-expired.

To help out during the locomotive shortage, a Peckett 'X2' class 0-6-0ST was

transferred to Desford in June 1965. Th engine had previously worked at Sout Leicester Colliery where it had bee named – somewhat appropriately SOUTH LEICESTER No.1, but rail traffi at that colliery had ceased in 1964 and following repairs, it was drafted t Desford. On arrival at Desford it wa steamed, but further repairs prove necessary (while being repaired it wa also repainted unlined green); as thing turned out, Desford's Austerity returne to traffic in September 1965 so th Peckett never actually had any regula work at its new home.

By now, however, the decision had bee taken to switch to diesel operatior DESFORD No.3 and SOUTI LEICESTER No.1 were transferred t Nailstone Colliery in 1966, an DESFORD went to Cashmore's for scra in June 1967. Seemingly no tears wer shed over the disappearance of stean Despite the fact that the engines wer well cared for in terms of bot maintenance and cleanliness, they wer apparently not regarded with any undu degree of affection or attachment, th prevailing attitude of the crews being tha it was 'just a job'.

All diesel

The first of the new breed of diesel arrived at Desford in 1966 – they came i the form of a pair of new 260hp Hunsle 0-6-0 diesel-hydraulics. However, thes locomotives were a new design an suffered from serious transmissio problems in their early years with th result that other locomotives had to b drafted in to cover during lengthy repairs. A similar 260hp Hunslet diesel was transferred from Whitwick Colliery at Coalville in June 1968 (though it stayed at Desford for less than a year), and a further one was transferred from Newdigate Colliery in 1970. The one from Newdigate, W/No.6693, was on hire to the NCB at the time – it had been the last of the batch and had initially proved unsaleable – but it was eventually purchased by the NCB for a very reasonable price.

Immediately prior to 6693's arrival at Desford the situation there had been so desperate that a Ruston & Hornsby 0-4-0 diesel-electric had had to be borrowed from Ellistown Colliery for seven weeks, but it had proved to be far too underpowered and, as soon as it could be spared, it had been returned to Ellistown with a polite 'thank you'. There are reports of two other Ruston diesels – 434024 of 1961 and 420138 of 1958 – having put in brief appearances at Desford but the dates are unknown and confirmation has been impossible to obtain. Another report for which confirmation is frustratingly lacking is that Donisthorpe Colliery's Hawthorn Leslie 0-6-0ST PHOENIX No.2 had a stint at Desford in 1967/68. If that is so, one can only imagine that it was there as cover while one or more of the diesels were out of action. Whatever the case, the engine was despatched to Cashmore's for scrap in August 1968, though as if to add further doubt to its presence at Desford, it went to its grave from Donisthorpe, not from Desford.

A locomotive which made only a relatively brief – but confirmed! – appearance at Desford was Rolls Royce 0-6-0 diesel-hydraulic 10212 which came from Measham Colliery in March 1971.

It left for Nailstone in June 1972 in exchange for English Electric 0-6-0 diesel-hydraulic D1200, which remained at Desford until August 1975.

As will be seen in the accompanying table the only other locomotive to see service at Desford was Ruston & Hornsby 0-4-0 diesel-hydraulic 544875 which was there from November 1975 until August 1984. However, that stint at Desford was not unbroken as the engine spent the period between July 1980 and August 1981 at Cadley Hill Colliery. On its return to Desford in August 1981 it joined Hunslets 6289 and 6693. It fell to this trio to hold the fort at Desford during the colliery's final years.

The last few years
In 1966 Merrylees was connected underground to Desford and the two were 'merged' as one operational unit. Hitherto Merrylees had sometimes been managed as a separate entity from Desford. Merrylees coal was subsequently taken underground by conveyor belt to Desford and its own surface rail link became redundant. In 1969 the Merrylees reserves were exhausted and the men were transferred to the Desford workings. The Merrylees drifts were subsequently used for ventilation and pumping purposes until September 1983 when they were sealed off.

In 1969 it was decided that the New Main seam, worked at other Leicestershire collieries, should be tapped into at Desford from No.2 shaft. No problems had been encountered with this seam elsewhere but at Desford heating occurred and in April 1971 a fire broke out. The fire was serious enough to threaten the future of the colliery before it was brought under control.

The steam winding engines at Desford were replaced in 1975/76 by electric engines from two closed collieries – Glapwell (N. Derbyshire) and Cannock Wood (Staffordshire) – but one boiler was retained for heating purposes. The replacement of the steam winding engines was rather late in the day, their longevity seemingly having been due to their efficiency. Certainly, one of the colliery engineers described them as 'fantastic machines'.

Although the colliery's 'output per manshift' figure increased during the early 1970s, somewhat perversely the actual manpower and overall output steadily declined. By the mid-1970s the coal reserves that could be worked at a profit were shrinking rapidly and closure was considered inevitable. Closure came on 10 February 1984.

By the time of Desford's closure only two locomotives were left there. One of the Hunslets, 6289, had been dispensed with in April 1983; it had been transferred to Snibston Colliery but, after finishing work there in 1986, it was saved for preservation by Leicestershire Museums. The two remaining engines at Desford in February 1984 were the other Hunslet, 6693, which stayed until 30 July 1984 when it, too, went to Snibston, and the Ruston, which remained on site until August 1984 when it was sold for scrap.

Epilogue
For those with a penchant for 'Then and Now', the site of Desford Colliery has been cleared, landscaped and converted into a conservation area. The only indication of its earlier history is the readily recognisable shape of the spoil heap which no amount of landscaping could disguise. Apart from that there are two concrete

DESFORD No.2 stands in the stock yard on 21 August 1949. The front coupling looks dangerously overlong and the smokebox door shows every sign of being burnt. Note the Fox wagon to the left. Fox were coal factors of Derby and operated all over the country. They probably acted as colliery agents too, as, pre-war, full trains of Fox wagons would leave the colliery for Leicester Power Station. Their wagons were black with white lettering and red shading. PHOTOGRAPH: F.A.WYCHERLEY COLLECTION

The Hunslet Austerity stands in front of the shed on 28 August 1954. It has not been possible to establish the function of the (very clean and tidy) wooden staging – it might have been used for coaling, although the usual practice was for the engines to be coaled directly from wagons. It has been suggested that it might have been for cleaning and/or maintenance purposes, but that is a rather tentative suggestion. **PHOTOGRAPH: DAVID DALTON; COURTESY JOHN BONSER**

markers showing the location of the two shafts, though you need to be an intrepid jungle explorer to find them now. A wheel has been installed on an island in the middle of a large pool, but this originates from Bagworth and not from Desford Colliery. (And the fishing rights to the pool belong to the ex Bagworth miners as well!) The only other indication of the previous existence of a colliery is that rich, pungent, unmistakable aroma of sulphur that catches the nostrils from time to time on hotter days.

Acknowledgements: The writer must record his great indebtedness to Tom Boulton, a former Desford collieryman, without whose generous help this article could never have been written. It was a privilege and a pleasure to be invited into his home and to listen to his recollections of

The Bagnall 0-4-0ST, photographed in the yard on 5 September 1946 very shortly after arrival at Desford. At its former place of work – ROF Rearsby – it had carried a nameplate R.O.F. 10, hence the bare patch on the tank. It was meant to be named MERRYLEES while at Desford, but it never received its new name. The building on the left is the engine shed, its smoke vent section seemingly in somewhat parlous condition. **PHOTOGRAPH: F.A.WYCHERLEY COLLECTION**

DESFORD No.2 on 14 May 1965. It has a different dome to the one seen in our earlier photograph. Externally, the state of the loco is remarkably good – as it was of all the others at Desford. All the engines there were painted in various shades of green, lined out in yellow and black (at least in the later years), except for No.2 which looked very smart in a coat of unlined dark green (including the wheels) with red coupling rods, red sides to the running plates and red sander levers. PHOTOGRAPH: R.C.RILEY; THE TRANSPORT TREASURY

an age that has now gone for ever. Grateful thanks are also owed to Eric Brown and, in particular, to Frank Gregory and Brian Hinsley, all former Desford men, especially for underground details, to Tony Overton for details of railway workings in the last 20 years and his generous provision of track diagrams and photographs, and to Roy Etherington for his kind perusal of and advice on the text and equally generous provision of additional information on the railway side.

Right. An internal side tipping steel wagon (made by Robert Hudson of Leeds?) stands in the sidings opposite the signal box. It had previously been used to take slack to the boilers but by the time this picture was taken on 30 July 1977 only one boiler was still working, so it is probably full of waste of some sort which has been left there fairly indefinitely awaiting disposal. PHOTOGRAPH: MIKE CHRISTENSEN

Top right. A relaxed Joe Underwood is in charge of a Becorit train carrying p props and a couple of miners. Note that the two wires along the roof were sti used by the 'guard' on this system too for signalling his requirements. Howeve all the manriders had a separate braking system in case of overspeed due t malfunction or rope breakage. Here the two box-like units at the front wer integrated with one another, one containing a centrifugal hydraulic brakin system which held the brakes off, the other a centrifugal overspeeder syste which cut in and applied the brakes if the speed got too high. On one wel remembered occasion a scientist turned up from Bretby to test the efficiency the braking unit. It was recommended that he sit in the back car with h equipment but this suggestion was superciliously dismissed and he insisted o sitting at the front. On a steep downwards incline speed was allowed to pick u quite rapidly and then the braking system was operated with some severit Some time later the scientist was still collecting his rather battered equipmer from the track some yards ahead of the train. A water pipe figures again on th right. Note also the untidy arrangement of struts about four feet up the girde on the left. They were triangular steel bars which slotted into the girders to kee them in place. PHOTOGRAPH: COURTESY M.CONIBEAR

Below. The Becorit trapped rail system, here operated by endless rope haulage, had been introduced by the end of the 1960s. This is believed to be a salvage train carrying pit props, split bars and at least one cable reel on the rear cars and sundry items of scrap in the leading car. The 6-inch square chock blocks on the left are supporting a water pipe which was there for the suppression of dust and in case of fire. PHOTOGRAPH: COURTESY M.CONIBEAR

This is the 2ft gauge track that ran for ¾-mile from the bottom of No.2 shaft. The train, an early (1963) manrider operated by endless rope haulage, is probably on an inspection trip. Joe Goode, on the left, is the 'guard' and on the right is the Colliery Manager, Reg Price (1960-71). The gentleman with the moustache is Martin Ryan who later became the President of the Leicestershire Area NUM. Competitions were held for safety slogans each month, and some of the posters featuring these appear on the wall. Note the siding on the right. PHOTOGRAPH: COURTESY M.CONIBEAR

The date is 25 April 1979, and 260hp Hunslet diesel W/No.6693 brings an MGR train up from the exchange sidings. It is taking it to the headshunt prior to propelling it back under the screens. We have a good view of the concrete head gear. PHOTOGRAPH: ADRIAN BOOTH

Later years at Desford – this picture was taken on 10 February 1979. The building on the left is the engine shed. PHOTOGRAPH: ADRIAN BOOTH

Another view of Hunslet W/No.6693 on 25 April 1979. We can see the fuelling tank where the water tank had originally stood just outside the shed. PHOTOGRAPH: ADRIAN BOOTH

IRISH INTERLUDE – EPISODE ONE

Photographs by Douglas Robinson; both taken in March 1959

These two wonderfully atmospheric pictures were taken at Ballinamore, the locomotive headquarters of the 3ft gauge Cavan & Leitrim Railway. The upper picture shows the loco yard with its typical array of discarded bits and pieces, uncleared ash and a liberal helping of smoke wafting all over the place. A pair of 2-4-2Ts is prominent; the open wagons are presumably for loco coaling. The lower picture shows a wagon rebuild in progress in the repair shops at Ballinamore. Although heavy loco repairs had to be done at Inchicore, Ballinamore was very capable of heavy repairs and rebuilding of rolling stock.

IRISH INTERLUDE – EPISODE TWO

Photographs by Ivo Peters; both taken on 5 July 1950

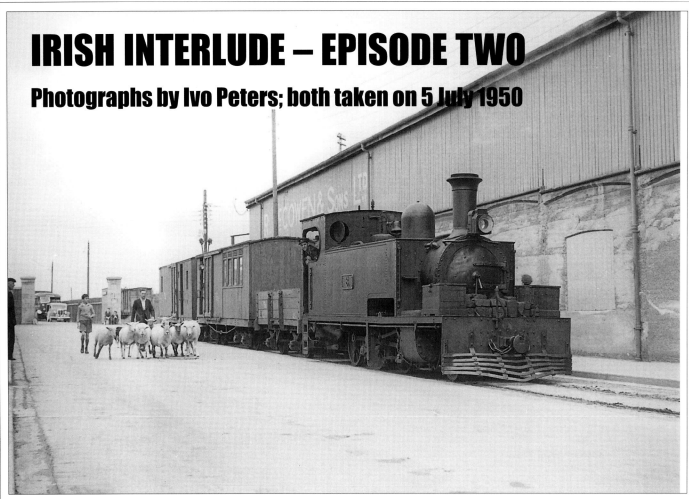

The Tralee & Dingle was another celebrated 3ft gauge system. In the upper picture T&D No.8T, one of the famous Hunslet 2-6-0Ts, trundles along the 'street tramway' section between the ex-GSWR broad gauge station at Tralee and the transfer yard at the old Tralee & Dingle terminus. The ex-GSWR premises are in the distance. May we make a request? No jokes about the flock of Manchester United supporters being led along the road, please. The lower picture shows Tralee shed with a pair of 2-6-0Ts outside and one inside. The former passenger platform is on the extreme right. The wagons in the yard are for cattle; the roofless ones had by this time been outlawed but there is plenty of photographic evidence that they were still regularly used by the T&D for the monthly cattle fairs at Dingle.

The article about the Chester-Ruthin line in the January 2000 edition of *Railway Bylines* (Vol.5 No.2) reminded me of a visit I made to part of the same stretch of railway on Thursday 18 September 1980. This was, of course, long after steam had finished, and the only section of the route which remained open was that between Penyffordd, on the Wrexham-Shotton line, and the Synthite Sidings on the Denbigh side of the former Mold station. (Synthite Sidings were some ¾ mile to the west of Mold station; they served the British Synthite Company which made, among other things, formaldehyde and solvents.)

That day I was in luck. Shortly after my arrival at Penyffordd station I made a judicious enquiry of the signalman regarding the freight traffic in the area; he advised me that a train was, at that very moment, on its way from Wrexham to the Synthite Sidings. Wasting little time, I positioned myself alongside the branch at Padeswood and, after a short wait, Brush Class 25 25168 came into view hauling five chemical tanks.

It had been some weeks since a train had traversed the line. This was evidenced by the fact that the guard had some difficulty in unlocking the level crossing gates at Llong – this caused quite a delay before the train could progress any farther. Later, and after depositing its wagons at the Synthite sidings, 25168 returned to Penyffordd and Wrexham with a couple of tanks.

When comparing my photographs taken at Llong and Mold in September 1980 to those from the 1950s and '60s (which featured in *Bylines 5:2*), it is clear that some further rationalisation had taken place in the intervening years. Alas, even the 'basic railway' which I had seen lasted for only a little longer. The last train to the Synthite Sidings ran on 15 March 1983 and, in December of that year, the line was truncated at Padeswood Cement Works. Today, Llong and Mold are consigned to history.

Right. OK – a Class 25 might not be the epitome of a 'Bylines' locomotive, but we're looking at an out-of-the-way section of railway which, by the time these pictures were taken, was 'goods only' and had already been partly-closed. So I rest my case that the actual railway is very much bona fide *Bylines* fare. We are looking at 25168 at Padeswood on its way to the Synthite Sidings at Mold.

Below right. Passing through Llong station which had closed to passengers in April 1962 – a little over eighteen years before this picture was taken. Compare this to the scene depicted on page 56 of *Bylines 5:2*.

Below. The train approaches the level crossing at Llong. The padlock on the gates had partly rusted up through disuse and was a so-and-so to open.

A postscript
CHESTER TO RUTHIN
--well, not quite to Ruthin

By Tom Heavyside

The train passes through Mold station which also closed to passengers in April 1962. The picture on page 57 of *Bylines 5:2* shows the station in a somewhat more intact condition with buildings on the up platform (on the left) and a footbridge.

On its return trip from the Synthite Sidings to Penyffordd and Wrexham, 25168 waits for the crossing gates to be opened at Llong.

For our final look at 25168 with the Synthite Sidings train on 18 September 1980 we return to Mold. This is the return working from the sidings approaching Mold station.

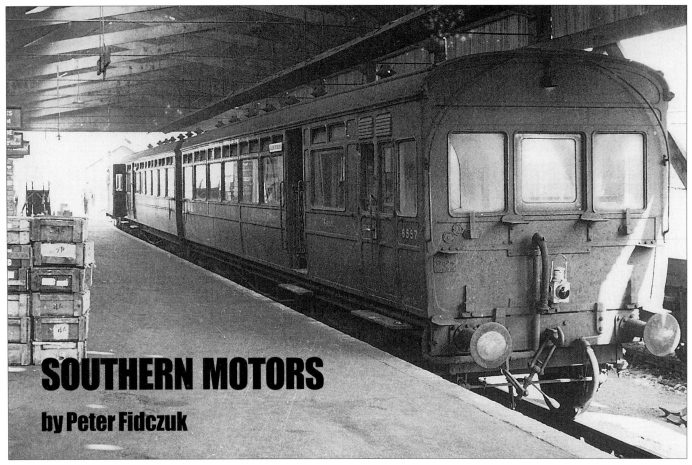

SOUTHERN MOTORS

by Peter Fidczuk

Starting in 1905 a number of railway companies developed push-pull trains – or motor trains or auto trains as they were alternatively referred to by different companies. Push-pulls were, in effect, a spin-off of steam railmotors. Although the railmotors had been very successful in many spheres of operation, one of their problems was that the locomotive portion and the carriage could not be easily separated for maintenance; this of course meant that if the locomotive portion needed attention the whole unit had to be taken out of service. The push-pull concept circumvented this handicap as the locomotive and carriage could be easily separated when necessary. Most importantly, push-pull trains retained one hugely useful feature of railmotors – they could be driven from the 'carriage' end, which meant that the engine did not have to run round at each end of the journey. This was particularly useful on smartly timed urban services where a very quick turn-round was required. Somewhat perversely, push-pull workings eventually became more commonplace on rural branch lines than in urban environments. Push-pulls remained a feature of railway operations until 1965, the very last being on the Seaton-Stamford line on the Rutland/Lincolnshire border.

On the Southern Railway, one of its three principal constituents – the LB&SCR – had been very quick off the mark and had introduced motor trains in 1905. Of the other principal constituents, the LSWR had introduced motor trains in 1906 and the SE&CR in 1912. The LB&SCR and the SE&CR both used compressed air control for their

motor trains, but the LSWR used a Heath-Robinsonesque system of cables and pulleys. It might be thought that, following the Grouping, the Southern Railway would have been keen to standardise the method of motor train control. But no. The Western Section (the ex-LSWR area) seemed set to retain the old cable and pulley system, but in 1929, following some potentially dangerous malfunctions of the equipment, it was decided to abandon the pulley and cable system and replace it with the compressed air system. Thus the latter became standard on all of the SR. And while we're on the subject of standardisation, it should be noted that, although the Southern Railway push-pulls were most commonly known as motor trains, the 'official' SR terminology was 'pull-and-push'. In BR days the 'official' term was 'push-and-pull'!

As for the coaches used for motor train workings, the Southern and its predecessors had the same policy as other railway companies in that most of the coaches used for motor train work were surplus or fairly elderly vehicles which had been adapted. Purpose-built sets were definitely in the minority. Although ex-LSWR coaches seemed to be the SR's preferred raw material for conversion, especially in the 1930s and '40s, coaches from the other constituent companies were also used. As the years progressed the coaches' adherence to home territory diminished so one could find, for example, ex-LSWR coaches working motor trains in Kent and ex-SE&CR vehicles working in Devon.

Obviously, this brief feature is not intended as an all-encompassing history of Southern motor train stock – such a

study would occupy several hefty tomes. Instead, we take a brief look at a random handful of coaches which have been selected for no other reason than the fact that the photographs looked rather interesting. We hope you agree.

Most of the photographs on these pages once formed part of the vast Lens of Sutton collection. Following John Smith's untimely death in 1999 they were acquired by the appropriately-titled 'Lens of Sutton Association' who can be contacted at 8 Smith's Farm Lane, Didcot, Oxon OX11 7DL. We imagine that an s.a.e. would be regarded as a common courtesy.

Above. We kick off with 6557, the driving brake composite of Set 366. This vehicle started life in 1905 as the coach portion of LSWR steam railmotor No.4 and, when the railmotor was withdrawn from service in 1919, the coach portion was converted to a push-pull trailer. (This was a very common fate for the coach portions of steam railmotors, not only on the SR constituent companies but on most railways throughout Britain.) And so 6557 owes its rather unusual end windows to its origins. This picture was taken at Callington *circa* 1948/49 and, for those of you watching in black and white, the vehicle is painted Southern green. Not all of the trains on the Callington branch were push-pulls; some were ordinary 'hauled' trains and others ran as mixed trains which, with the requirement for the goods vehicles behind the passenger vehicles, made push-pull operation impossible. Nevertheless, 6557 lasted on the branch until April 1956; latterly it had usually run as a single coach PHOTOGRAPH: LENS OF SUTTON ASSOCIATION (61460)

This end-on view gives a good indication of the standard format used by the SR when converting existing passenger stock for push-pull working. Four large windows, footsteps to the lamp brackets, a wiper on the driver's right-hand window and two sand pipes to the leading wheels. The two hoses visible are the usual ones for the vacuum brake and stream heating but there were three additional hoses between the second coach and the loco which activated the compressed air regulator controls. The 1934 SR General Appendix described the hoses thus:

a)   Regulator control hose pipe (painted blue)
b)   Main storage hose pipe (painted green)
c)   Back pressure hose pipe (painted yellow)

There was also a cable with a three-pin coupling containing the regulator indicator and bell wires – there was a system of bell codes for communicating between the footplate and the driving compartment of the coach. The SR Appendix of 1934 gives only one code – one ring for opening or shutting the regulator. However, the instructions in BR days (as given in the 1960 Appendix) were:

• About to open or close the regulator from the driving compartment – 1 short
• Take brake off – 2 short
• Sound locomotive whistle – 3 short
• Reverse – 4 short
• Emergency stop – 1 long
• Shut main regulator – 2 long
• Open main regulator – 3 long
• Driver leaving driving compartment to carry out rules etc – 5 short

The vehicle we are looking at is S4053S which had started life in 1925 as a corridor brake third, built by the SR to the old LSWR 'Ironclad' design. As we can see, it was part of Set 382. This was one of four similar sets (381-384) which were converted for push-pull use on the Western Division in 1949. It was condemned in 1959. It is seen here at Lymington Pier probably fairly soon after conversion, in which case the livery is BR crimson with the set number in yellow.
PHOTOGRAPH: LENS OF SUTTON ASSOCIATION (61496)

Right. From the 1930s the Southern carried out a number of conversions of older stock for push-pull working by pairing existing vehicles with vehicles formed by rebuilding old coach bodies on to standard SR 58ft underframes. That method was used to form sets 1 to 6 in 1937: ex-LSWR 56ft lavatory brake composites were converted to driving brake composites and were paired with 'new' brake thirds which had been formed by rebuilding ex-LSWR 48ft composites on to new 58ft underframes and adding a steel-clad brake compartment. The driving brake compo nearest the camera here is S6488S which had been built in 1911 as a tri-composite brake; after conversion for push-pull working in 1937 it had been paired with rebuilt brake third 2620, but that vehicle was replaced in July 1958 by ex-SE&CR 100-seater third S1066S. This picture was taken at Poole. The set is on a Brockenhurst-Bournemouth West working sometime between July 1958 (when S1066S replaced S2620) and late 1961 (when Set No.1 was transferred to the Central Division). Set No.1 finally met its end in June 1962. PHOTOGRAPH: LENS OF SUTTON ASSOCIATION (61419)

Below left. In the introduction it was mentioned that ex-LSWR coaches seemed to be the preferred raw material for the SR rebuilds and conversions of the 1930s and 1940s, but sets 731 to 739 (of which the pictured set 738 is an example) had a more convoluted genesis undergoing two bouts of rebuilding by the SR. The origin of these sets was as LSWR 46ft 6in corridor coaches of a type known as 'Emigrant Stock'; so named as they were designed to transfer emigrants after arrival at any UK port to Southampton for departure to America. Surprisingly, these rather old coaches were re-engineered with new non-standard length SR underframes in 1935, and in early 1943 they embarked on another new lease of life when they were converted for push-pull service, retaining their original body length. In the conversion the end gangways were removed but the gangways between the coaches in the set were retained. S4763S was paired with S2648S in set 738 and lasted until June 1960. It is shown here at Uralite Halt on the Gravesend Central-Allhallows service on 4 May 1957; the sets in use on the line at this date (sets 735 and 737 were also commonly used) were painted crimson. Uralite Halt itself lay just beyond the junction with the main line at Hoo and served the adjacent Uralite asbestos works. Wagons in the extensive Hoo Junction marshalling yard are visible in the background. PHOTOGRAPH: FRANK GOUDIE; THE TRANSPORT TREASURY

'Make do and mend' is typified by brake composite 6406 which had been 'built' in 1937. Note the use of inverted commas for 'built'... The vehicle had a second-hand underframe which came from ex-LSWR 57ft 'Ironclad' corridor first 7180 which had been damaged in a fire at Micheldever. It was mounted on the massive Warner bogies which had been unique to the LSWR. The body was also second-hand; most of it came from a 48ft ex-LSWR composite to which was added a guard's compartment which, unusually, was constructed in similar panelling rather than steel sheeting. To form the push-pull set it was paired with ex-SE&CR 100 seat third 1057. The set remained intact until October 1956 when S6406S was condemned, but S1057S soldiered on as a 'solo' coach until 1961. This picture was taken inside the carriage shed at Stewarts Lane. The livery appears to be newly-applied Malachite Green with large class numerals on the doors. PHOTOGRAPH: LENS OF SUTTON ASSOCIATION (61424)

The LB&SC was an extensive user of push-pull trains and constructed a number of purpose-built sets. Initially they were of the usual LB&SC arc roof pattern; later ones were to the 'Balloon' design (so named because of their bulbous elliptical roof which was to the absolute limit of the LB&SC loading gauge) but, for the final ones, the design reverted to the low arc roof. The coach nearest the camera here – S3826 – was purpose-built in 1911 and paired with composite 6202. As Set 729 it lasted until 1960. Although these vehicles had an antiquated appearance, they were gangwayed within the set and had side corridors in each coach; given that they were only 8ft wide the compartments would have been very cramped, and so the 'corridor' was open-sided and the interior was more like that of an 'open' carriage (rather like a 4 SUB or 4 EPB open but with the gangway to the side instead of centrally). Set 729 was allocated to the Central Section from 1941 and was photographed at Hailsham on either a Tunbridge Wells West-Eastbourne service or more likely on one of the Hailsham-Eastbourne shuttles. Making up the four-coach ensemble (between this two-car set and the loco) is one of the 'Ironclad' conversions of 1937. PHOTOGRAPH: LENS OF SUTTON ASSOCIATION (61503)

We now move along to the Eastern Section which took in the old SE&CR area. The SE&CR had introduced railmotors in 1904/05 but they were not too successful and, in common with many other railway companies which found themselves in the same situation, when the railmotors were withdrawn the coach portions were converted for 'ordinary' usage. Four of the coach portions from the SE&CR railmotors were used to make two two-car push-pull sets; as such they originally went to the Isle of Wight but spent only two years on the island before coming back to the mainland. One of the sets was 482. It comprised motor driving third S3583S (nearer the camera) and third S915S which had been a composite until being downgraded in 1941. Most of the accommodation was in the form of open saloons but the two guard's compartments were deceptive as, when converted for push-pull work in 1924, the farther one was used for additional seating. Set 482 was regularly used on the Westerham branch in 1959/59, at which time the coaches were painted carmine. The train is seen on such a working at Dunton Green with an H Class 0 4 4T at the far end. By the time of their withdrawal in 1960 these coaches were most unusual in that, at only 48ft in length, they were very short; the recessed door and guard's compartment were also very unusual. PHOTOGRAPH: LENS OF SUTTON ASSOCIATION (61426)

Top left. The driving brake third of Set 661 was S3433S which had been built by the Metropolitan Amalgamated Carriage & Wagon Company in December 1913 as part of an SE&CR trio set. In its original guise it was a fully panelled 60ft birdcage brake third but, when converted for push-pull working in September 1942, it lost its observatory and, by the time this photograph was taken in 1957/58, it had also lost a great deal of its 'Gothic' panelling. Set 661 was originally used on the Crowhurst-Bexhill West branch (this picture was taken at Bexhill West), but after that branch was dieselised it was transferred to the Tunbridge Wells West-Oxted shuttles. It was condemned in October 1961. PHOTOGRAPH: LENS OF SUTTON ASSOCIATION (61442)

Above. By 1959 the Southern Region's motley collection of push-pull sets was getting rather long in the tooth – and that's putting it mildly! – so authorisation was given for the conversion of ten sets of Maunsell coaches, with an additional ten sets in 1960. These conversions, it was envisaged, would see out the end of steam-worked push-pulls. The driving brake composites were all converted from corridor brake composites which had been built in 1935 – they had large flush panelled windows. The trailers had started life as open thirds in 1933. After conversion the twenty sets (600-619) all entered service in SR green. They bore a striking resemblance to the EPB electric sets which had been built during the 1950s, but this was not a coincidence as the driving compartments of the push-pull coaches were modelled on the 'Eastleigh' EMU cab. Set 610 is seen here at Westerham on 10 September 1961; it had replaced the ex-SE&CR railmotor set which featured in one of our earlier photographs. At the far end is H Class 0 4 4T 31518 which will propel the set back to Dunton Green as the 4.23pm. As for our Set 610, it had been formed in June 1960 and comprised driving brake composite S6679S and open second S1317S. The set was condemned in 1964. PHOTOGRAPH: JOHN SCRACE

Left. To round off this whistle-stop survey of Southern motor trains we have set 715 waiting at the bleak, windswept Lydd-on-Sea station with an early afternoon train from New Romney to Ashford on Saturday 7 June 1958. This station had opened in 1937 with high hopes of it having to deal with a good deal of traffic to and from holiday camps, homes and hotels. Although the camps later generated some traffic, the area – and with it, the station – never hit the heady heights that had once been anticipated. But we digress... The SE&CR steam railmotors had once worked on the New Romney branch so it seems fitting to end with another SE&CR set. However, as if to confirm that nothing was totally straightforward on the Southern, set 715 is not all what it seems – it had started life as an ex-LB&SC set! Its 'South Eastern-isation' (if you'll excuse the phraseology) began in 1941 when its composite was replaced by ex-SE&CR 5298, and in 1952 the driving brake third was replaced with S3475S, a brake third from a 60ft SE&CR trio set. Unlike the vehicle shown in set 661 (see above left), S3475S was built to a modernised design in 1921 and so never had an observatory; the panelling is also deceptive – it is wood not steel. Set 715 was condemned in March 1961. PHOTOGRAPH: J.H.ASTON

THE CRUDEN BAY HOTEL AND ITS TRAMWAY

One of the Cruden Bay Hotel tramcars, photographed when brand new in 1899 and resplendent in full GNSR livery. The uniformed hotel staff pose proudly for the photographer; the driver manages to look quite menacing. PHOTOGRAPH: COURTESY THE GRAMPIAN TRANSPORT MUSEUM

Until the early 1860s the only means of land travel between Aberdeen and Peterhead was by the turnpike road by way of Ellon, Hatton and the Parish of Cruden, public transport on that route being provided by the *Mail* and the *Defiance* coaches. However, that changed in July 1862 when the Formartine & Buchan Railway (a nominally independent company but, in effect, a subsidiary of the Great North of Scotland Railway) opened its line from Dyce, via Ellon, Maud and Mintlaw to Peterhead. With the coming of the railway the road coaches were discontinued, but this displeased the residents of Hatton, Cruden and Boddam as they had been deprived of their one and only direct link to Aberdeen. The residents regularly lobbied the GNSR to provide a railway link and, over the years, a number of proposals – including one for a steam worked tramway – were put forward. But nothing happened for more than thirty years.

Eventually – in 1893 – the GNSR obtained parliamentary powers for a railway from Ellon to Boddam with intermediate stations at Auchmacoy, Pitlurg, Hatton, Cruden Bay (this station served the village of Port Erroll, but was located adjacent to the popular Bay of Cruden) and Longhaven. The construction of the line commenced in 1894 and it was finally opened to the

public in 1897. An excursion train ran to Ellon on Saturday 31 July of that year and the line opened to the public the following Monday, the 2nd August. A halt opened at Bullers o' Buchan in 1899, principally for visitors to the locally well-known coastal rock formation and beauty spot. Whereas the new line to Boddam pleased the residents of certain villages, it displeased many of the folk of Peterhead. The terminus of the new line at Boddam was only about 2½ miles from Peterhead, and there was a strong feeling in Peterhead that the line should have been extended, thereby providing a

by Keith Jones

considerably shorter route between Peterhead and Aberdeen. But it was not to be.

Diversification
By the latter part of the 1800s the GNSR was diversifying into other areas of business, and in 1890 it obtained parliamentary powers to operate hotels. The company established a Hotel Committee to administer that aspect of its business. The GNSR's first hotel was the Palace Hotel in Union Street, Aberdeen; hitherto privately-owned, the GNSR took it over and renovated and

extended it. It reopened on 22 August 1891 and was an immediate success. This encouraged the GNSR to further expand into the hotel business; the

thinking was that not only would the hotels generate additional revenue, but they would also generate additional railway traffic.

In January 1895 the board decided to look into the possibility of building a luxury hotel near Port Erroll, on the Buchan coast. By the end of that month estimates and plans were submitted for the Port Erroll Hotel, as it was provisionally referred to. The original intention was that the hotel would have 55 bedrooms and would be built of pink Peterhead granite, the estimated cost of which was £13,816. The plan was generally approved, and the GNSR's engineer, Mr. Patrick Barnett, was instructed to provide drawings and specifications; these were prepared by the company's architect Mr. John J. Smith. The original plans were, however, revised, and the 'new' scheme was for a hotel with 75 bedrooms. The final estimates submitted in April 1896 reflected the considerable escalation of size and costs. The construction of the building was quoted at £16,000, lifts £650, heating £350, furnishings £4,000 and landscaping, walls etc £1,000 – a total cost of £21,000. But that was not all. The GNSR had originally hoped that the local district council would provide water and sewerage to the new hotel, but as things turned out the GNSR had to provide the services itself at an additional cost of £1,200. Lighting was originally intended to be by paraffin lamp, but the GNSR directors decided that '...if a laundry is erected, electric lighting can be provided at a probable outlay of £1,000 for dynamo and wiring...'

with an additional £400 for fittings. The bold step was taken to proceed with an electric power supply.

At some stage in the preliminary planning the title of the hotel was formally changed to the Cruden Bay Hotel. The contracts for the construction of the hotel and ancillary works were let to a number of contractors and sub-contractors, the largest contract for masonry work being awarded to Mr. Edgar Gauld of Aberdeen. Construction commenced in late 1896. Provisioning contracts were let for food supplies, wines, spirits, furnishings and such equipment as cutlery, crockery and glassware. The scale of the task of equipping the hotel can be seen by the contract awarded to James Allan and Sons, Union Street, Aberdeen for upholstery and furnishings. Reported as being one of the largest of its kind ever executed in Aberdeen, the contract involved nearly 400 chairs, 75 bedroom suites in walnut for the guest bedrooms, and 30 to 40 suites for the staff quarters. There were 110 beds, together with settees, tables, lounge suites, and 'some acres' (as the GNSR put it) of the finest Axminster carpeting.

Despite the considerable outlay on the hotel's interior comforts, the GNSR's directors had already envisaged that the hotel's major selling point would be, not inside, but outside. This exterior attraction took the form of a golf course –

or to be precise, two golf courses. Indeed, part of one course was playable in 1897, some two years before the hotel itself had been completed.

Some of the original development work at the hotel itself was undertaken by Miss McKilliam, the manageress of the Palace Hotel in Aberdeen. In September 1897 a Miss Duffus was appointed as the first permanent manageress at

This early aerial view confirms the impressive scale of the hotel. The main 'carriage entrance' is in the foreground – it is just about possible to make out the tramway tracks along the front of the building – while the laundry and workshops are in the top left of the picture. PHOTOGRAPH: COURTESY THE GRAMPIAN TRANSPORT MUSEUM

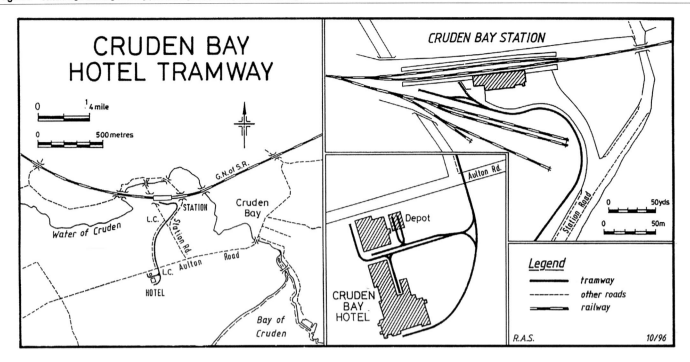

Cruden Bay, her salary being £100 per annum and her remit being to take charge of the equipping of the as-yet-unfinished hotel as from 1 January 1898. However, Miss Duffus resigned without taking office, and Miss Catherine Campbell of Brighton was appointed in her place. Miss Campbell remained in post only until January 1900.

It was reported in February 1898 that the construction work was well advanced and plastering work was in progress. The GNSR expressed hope that the hotel would be open for guests during that year.

However, there was still one important matter which had not yet been addressed, let alone resolved. This was the matter of the hotel's location, over half a mile away from Cruden Bay station. Given that the intention was to attract the 'top class of clientele', the GNSR's directors considered that they needed to offer a means of transportation – preferably incorporating the latest in creature comforts – between the station and the hotel. In August 1898 the GNSR's directors visited the Isle of Man to inspect the electric and light railways

there and, although that visit was intended principally to gather information for a possible light railway to the suburbs of Aberdeen, the delegation clearly considered that there was an alternative use for an electric tramway as, on 14 September 1898, the GNSR Board '…considered further plans for a laundry, a combined passenger and luggage lift, and an electrical tramway between the hotel and the station, including an extra engine and dynamo at Cruden Bay'. The cost was put at £9,005. It was decided to go ahead with the whole

The hotel dining room and staff in the 1930s. What a picture – all one needs are Emma Thompson and Helena Bonham-Carter to complete the scene. PHOTOGRAPH: COURTESY THE GRAMPIAN TRANSPORT MUSEUM

PRIVATE.

GREAT NORTH OF SCOTLAND RAILWAY.

WORKING TIME TABLES,

AUGUST, 1897.

The Working Time Tables for June, 1897, will continue in force from 1st August, and until further notice, with the following alterations, namely :—

BUCHAN SECTION.

9·25 a.m. Train from Aberdeen will call at Arnage at 10·16 a.m., and will be due to leave Auchnagatt and Stations beyond 3 minutes later than shewn in Time Table Book.

CRUDEN SECTION.

Opening of New Line from Ellon to Boddam.

The New Cruden Line between Ellon and Boddam will be opened on Monday, 2nd August for Goods and Passenger Traffic, and Trains are to be worked upon it in conformity with the Company's Rules and Regulations according to the annexed Time Table.

Miles from Ellon.	FROM: ELLON TO BODDAM—DOWN TRAINS. STATIONS.	1 Pass.	2 Pass.	3 Goods	4 Pass.	5 Pass.	6 Goods	7 Pass.	Miles from Boddam.	FROM BODDAM TO ELLON—UP TRAINS. STATIONS.	1 Pass.	2 Goods	3 Pass.	4 Pass.	5 Goods	6 Pass.	7 Pass.
		a.m.	a.m.	a.m.	p.m.	p.m.	p.m.	p.m.			a.m.	a.m.	a.m.	p.m.	p.m.	p.m.	p.m.
..	Aberdeen...de.	8 10	9 25	5 40	12 40	4 5	4 45	6 50	..	Boddam...dep.	7 35	9 0	9 50	12 45	2 30	3 50	7 30
..	Fraserbro' ,,	7 0	9 25	7 30	...	3 35	1 40	7 0	2	Longhaven......	7 40	9 10	9 55	12 50	2 40	3 55	7 35
..	Peterhead ,,	7 15	9 30	8 15	..	3 40	2 0	7 10	5¼	Cruden {arr. {Bay {dep.	...	9 20					
..											7 48	9 30	10 3	12 58	2 57	4 3	7 43
3½	Ellon ......dep.	8 55	10 45	11 0	1 40	5 10	6 40	8 20	..	Hatton......	7 54	9 41	10 9	1 4	3 10	4 9	7 49
5½	Auchmacoy......	9 3	10 53	11 17	1 48	5 18	6 57	7¼	Pitlurg......	8 0	9 52	10 15	1 10	3 22	4 15	7 55
8½	Pitlurg	9 9	10 59	11 30	1 54	5 21	7 10	8 34	10	Auchmacoy	8 6	10 4	10 21	1 16	3 35	4 21	8 1
8½	Hatton	9 15	11 5	11 42	2 0	5 30	7 22	8 40	12½	Ellon...... arr.	8 15	10 15	10 30	1 25	3 47	4 30	8 10
10½	Cruden Bay......	9 22	11 12	11 57	2 7	5 37	7 43	8 47	15½								
13½	Longhaven......		9 29	11 19	12 12	2 14	5 44	7 57	8 54	..	Peterhead ar.	9 55	4p20	..	2 40	8 10	6 10	..
15½	Boddam...... arr.		9 35	11 25	12 20	2 20	5 50	8. 5	9 0	..	Fraserbro' ,,	9 55	4 40	..	2 50	8 37	6 20	..
										..	Aberdeen ,,	9 20	12 20	11 30	3 20	6 11	5 20	9 10

Train Crossings Stations.

DOWN TRAINS—
No. 1 Down 8·55 a.m. Train crosses 9·0 a.m. Up Goods Train at Cruden Bay.
No. 6 Down 6·40 p.m. Goods Train crosses 7·30 p.m. Up Train at Cruden Bay.

UP TRAINS—
No. 2 Up 9·0 a.m. Goods Train crosses 8·55 a.m. Down Train at Cruden Bay.
No. 5 Up 2·30 p.m. Goods Train crosses 1·40 p.m. Down Train at Boddam.
No. 7 Up 7·30 p.m. Train crosses 6·40 p.m. Down Goods Train at Cruden Bay.

Notes of Working.

The Goods Trains are to work Goods Traffic with all Stations as required.

Please acknowledge receipt immediately to Superintendent.

W. MOFFATT, *General Manager.*

ABERDEEN, 23rd July, 1897.

...scheme, including the tramway ...provided that satisfactory arrangements can be made for the necessary land...and for crossing the road'. This appeared to cause no problem, as Aberdeen County Council agreed to the line crossing the Newburgh-Port Erroll road on three conditions: firstly that the GNSR accepted full accident liability, secondly that the company paved the road between the rails and for four feet on either side, and thirdly that the County Council could revoke their permission at any time.

The hotel opened with some ceremony and with much attention from the local press on 1 March 1899, the GNSR directors and their party travelling by special train to Cruden Bay station. The station itself, although constructed of wood, had been built in a style to complement the hotel, with glass canopies, first and second class waiting rooms and a refreshment room.

The tramway

Although Cruden Bay Hotel had opened in March 1899, the tramway between Cruden Bay station and the hotel was not ready until about mid-June. The line itself was constructed very much as a railway and was built on a private right of way. The track was bullhead rail on chaired sleepers, with open ballasted formation between the main road crossing and the station yard. At the hotel and within the station yard, the track was paved to rail level with granite setts. The gauge was a nominal 3ft 6½in.

Starting from the railway station, a short loop with a siding was laid to the west of the station building. The line then followed the western edge of the station approach road, entered a shallow cutting by the side of the Hatton-Port Erroll road and then crossed a field. It finally crossed the Newburgh-Port Erroll road before entering the hotel grounds, passed round the front of the hotel, then terminated by the front door. A triangular junction just over the road crossing led to a branch to the two-track car shed and laundry. Access to the car shed and the west side of the laundry was by means of a turntable.

The rolling stock consisted of two single-deck four-wheel tramcars, a four-wheel van, an open four-wheel trailer for coal and two additional four-wheel bogies for carrying boilers or other heavy items. All the rolling stock was built at the GNSR's Kittybrewster works, with the exception of the tramcar trucks (the underframe and wheels) which were of the Peckham 'Excelsior' type 7B. The trucks had a 6ft 6in wheelbase, 2ft 6in diameter wheels and a 15hp motor. The bodies were of a clerestoried 'combination' type. The passenger compartments had longitudinal seating for sixteen persons occupying three window bays. The equivalent of a fourth bay was provided by a gated platform area for conveying luggage and laundry baskets. The passenger accommodation was particularly luxurious in that it had comfortable, upholstered seating and matching curtains. Extensive use was made of wrought ironwork and etched and bevelled glass; the passenger doors of wood and glass were particularly ornate. The controllers were of an unusual vertical type, probably manufactured by the GNSR itself. An electric headlight and a bulb type warning horn were fitted at each end, and the passenger compartment was electrically lit. The tramcars were originally painted in green and cream, probably with purple lake dashboard. They were also fully lined out, with CRUDEN BAY HOTEL in block shaded letters.

The power supply was from a 33kw combined vertical Bellis & Morcom engine and Parker generator located in the hotel's boiler house. It was

A full-frontal of the hotel – if you'll pardon the terminology – in GNSR days. One of the trramcars waits outside the entrance. PHOTOGRAPH: GNSRA COLLECTION

distributed by copper wire suspended from tramway type bracket arms, again heavily decorated with wrought iron. That said, it appears that the electricity supply was not completed in time for the opening of the tramway; it is believed that the tramcars were hauled by horses for a few months until power was available.

The tramcars were originally kept in the open. It was not until mid-July 1899 that the GNSR's Finance Committee resolved to provide a shed for the cars at a cost of £500.

Fares were not charged for hotel guests, but non-residents paid 3d, plus 3d for luggage. During high summer, monthly receipts in 1899 and 1900 were upwards of £16. Off-season it was minimal.

Golf

Mention was made earlier of the golf courses at the hotel. The GNSR's publicity for the hotel enthusiastically trumpeted the 'healthy climate' and 'bracing air', but it also keenly promoted the golf courses. There were two courses, one of 18 holes and one of 9 holes, the latter being known as the 'St.Olaf Course' or 'Ladies Course'. No expense had been spared by the GNSR to make the golf courses as perfect as possible, and with this in mind the distinguished designer Thomas Morris of St.Andrews had been employed. As already mentioned, part of the new course was playable in 1897;

nine holes were in use during 1898. Alex N.Weir was appointed first Golf Professional at a salary of £70 during the first season; he also acted as chief green-keeper and club-maker. The Cruden Bay Hotel was the first of the railway-owned hotels to be based around a golf course and what today would be known as 'leisure facilities'. It preceded the Caledonian Railway's Gleneagles Hotel by a quarter of a century.

The first of many major tournaments was held on 14 and 15 April 1899. They attracted many of the day's leading players, including the Open Champion, Harry Vardon, who won the first prize of £30.

In 1920 the GNSR again approached the leading golf course designers of the day – by this time the sought-after 'names' were Tom Simpson and his assistant Herbert Fowler – to redesign the courses to modern standards. The redesigned courses, completed in 1926, were sometimes regarded as one of Tom Simpson's finest projects. He retained a strong connection with the Cruden Bay Golf Club and was its Honorary President until his death in 1964.

Hotel business

The hotel results for the first five months of operation were described by the GNSR as '...most encouraging', and as a result the tariff was revised upwards for August and September 1899. A sitting room on the first floor now cost £6 for a week of

seven days. Full board comprised 'Bath and light, Breakfast, Luncheon, Afternoon Tea and Dinner'. Fires in individual rooms, billiards, bicycle storage, laundry and, of course, golf were extra.

From the outset the hotel succeeded in attracting Britain's rich and famous. The guest list included Sir Jeremiah Colman (of mustard fame), Sir James Burrell whose art collection is now housed in a purpose built gallery in Glasgow, Sir Eric Hambro of the banking family, Lloyd George and Herbert Asquith, the American millionaire Pierpoint Morgan, the famous contralto Clara Butt and her husband Kennerley Rumford. Very many members of the British business community, judiciary and aristocracy also stayed at the hotel. Although his favourite holiday residence was the nearby *Kilmarnock Arms Hotel* another occasional guest at Cruden Bay was the theatre manager and author Bram Stoker, whose *Dracula* is said to have been inspired by the mystical appearance of the nearby Slains Castle, the family seat of the Earls of Erroll.

The hotel depended for most of its existence on seasonal employees and retained only a skeleton permanent staff to look after those hardy guests who braved a Buchan winter. Although the summer was invariably busy – accommodation within the hotel was always at a premium – the holiday season was short. Consequently, despite

GREAT NORTH OF SCOTLAND RAILWAY

OPENING OF THE
CRUDEN RAILWAY.

On MONDAY, 2ND AUGUST, 1897.

THE PASSENGER TRAIN SERVICE WILL BE AS FOLLOWS :—

		A.M.	A.M.	P.M.	P.M.	P.M.
Aberdeen	dep.	8·10	9·25	12·40	4 5	6·50
Fraserburgh	,,	7·0	9·25	—	3·35	7·0
Peterhead	,,	7·15	9 30	—	3·40	7·10
Ellon	dep.	8·55	10·45	1·40	5·10	8·20
Auchmacoy	,,	9·3	10·53	1·48	5·18	8·28
Pitlurg	,,	9·9	10·59	1·54	5·24	8·34
Hatton	,,	9·15	11·5	2·0	5·30	8·40
Cruden Bay	,,	9·22	11·12	2·7	5·37	8·47
Longhaven	,,	9·29	11·19	2·14	5·44	8·54
Boddam	arr.	9·35	11·25	2·20	5·50	9·0

		A.M.	A.M.	P.M.	P.M.	P.M.
Boddam	dep.	7·35	9·50	12·45	3·50	7·30
Longhaven	,,	7·40	9·55	12·50	3·55	7·35
Cruden Bay	,,	7·48	10·3	12·58	4·3	7·43
Hatton	,,	7·54	10·9	1·4	4·9	7·49
Pitlurg	,,	8·0	10·15	1·10	4·15	7·55
Auchmacoy	,,	8·6	10·21	1·16	4·21	8·1
Ellon	,,	8·15	10·30	1·25	4·30	8·10
Peterhead	arr.	9·55	—	2·40	6·10	—
Fraserburgh	,,	9·55	—	2·50	6·20	—
Aberdeen	,,	9·20	11·30	3·20	5·20	9·10

There will also be a regular service of Trains for Goods, Live Stock, and Fish Traffic.

Information as to Fares, Rates, Times of Goods Trains, &c., may be obtained on application to Mr A. G. REID, Passenger Superintendent, Aberdeen; Mr A. M. ROSS, Goods Manager, Aberdeen; or to the STATION AGENTS.

The Company's NEW HOTEL at CRUDEN BAY is expected to be ready for the Season of 1898.

W. MOFFATT, General Manager.

CRUDEN RAILWAY.

'BUSES will run between PETERHEAD and BODDAM in connection with all trains, leaving Peterhead 35 minutes before departure of trains.

JAMES REID & SON,
Peterhead, August, 1897.

NOTICE.

IN connection with CRUDEN RAILWAY a CONVEYANCE for the convenience of passengers will ply between PETERHEAD and BODDAM, leaving BROAD STREET 35 minutes before specified times of departures of trains, and returning with passengers from each train.

JAMES SUTHERLAND.
Horse Hirer, etc.

NOTICE TO CREDITORS.

As Mr GEORGE WRIGHT, Gardener, South Toll Bar, has DISPOSED of his BUSINESS as a

---

the hotel's promising start its income was less than the company had originally anticipated. This, of course, was a source of displeasure to the GNSR's shareholders. In the early years the hotel regularly failed to meet annual running costs, let alone make a decent return on capital. There was a considerable turnover of managers – Miss Campbell had been succeeded in 1900 by Miss Frater who, in 1902, was herself succeeded by a Mr. Trenchard – and in 1906 the company decided to offer the hotel for let. Several major hotel and catering companies were invited to submit bids, but nothing came of it and the hotel therefore remained with the GNSR.

Fortuitously, as it turned out, later in 1906 the GNSR appointed a Miss Williams as manageress; she had previously held a similar position at a Carnoustie hotel. Miss Williams' salary at Cruden Bay was £100 per annum plus 2½% of the profits. Under Miss Williams' guidance the hotel's income and expenditure were stabilised and the establishment started to make a modest profit. Miss Williams also retained the confidence of the GNSR board, and this resulted in her remaining at Cruden Bay (apart from a short period as acting manageress of the Palace at Aberdeen) until the demise of the GNSR at the Grouping in 1923.

By the early 1920s the principal form of transport for many of the hotel's guests was the motor car. The hotel kept up with trends. It was 'approved' by the Scottish Automobile Club, and could offer not only garage accommodation for the cars, but also sleeping accommodation for the chauffeurs.

LNER days
At the Grouping in 1923 the GNSR and its assets – including the Cruden Bay Hotel – became part of the LNER. During Miss Williams' time as manageress at Cruden Bay her book-keeper, Miss Allan, had occasionally deputised for her, and when Miss Williams retired in 1923 Miss Allan was appointed as her successor. Miss Allan remained in post until her retirement in 1932.

The Cruden Bay Hotel was, of course, just one of several quality hotels which the LNER inherited from its constituent companies. The LNER continued to attract wealthy guests to the hotel and invested in hot and cold running water in all bedrooms. In 1939 the decision was taken to provide *en suite* facilities in many rooms, but this was overtaken by world events.

The hotel tramway also passed into LNER hands in 1923. The main change of the post-Grouping era was the adoption of the LNER's varnished teak livery for the tramcars. As far as can be determined one tram was kept in pristine condition for guest use, the other being used for laundry and goods haulage services.

Going back to the early 1930s, there were changes on the main line railway serving Cruden Bay. The Boddam branch had always been a lossmaker, especially after the introduction of frequent parallel bus services to Aberdeen, principally provided by Messrs Sutherland of Peterhead. From January 1931 the already sparse service of passenger trains on the branch was further reduced to just two trains in each direction. They usually consisted of an elderly 4-4-0 locomotive, a third class and a composite carriage and a passenger brake van. As a further economy the passing loops at the intermediate stations were removed and the signalling staff were redeployed elsewhere. Notwithstanding this downgrading, the LNER decided to repaint Cruden Bay station. However, this turned out to be something of a disaster as, on 23 April 1931, a painter's blow torch set fire to the main station building. It was totally destroyed. Fortunately, it was possible to use the

Cruden Bay tramcar No.1 at the hotel in early LNER days. The two golfers are senior LNER officers; there was a strong interest in golf among senior GNSR officers and their successors on the LNER, so 'fact finding' missions to golfing hotels were no doubt very welcome. PHOTOGRAPH: COURTESY THE GRAMPIAN TRANSPORT MUSEUM

Tramcar No.2 photographed in a sea mist – a not uncommon climatic condition at Cruden Bay – on 12 August 1937. By this time the tramway was used to convey goods only. PHOTOGRAPH: GNSRA COLLECTION

LONDON & NORTH EASTERN RAILWAY.

GENERAL MANAGER'S OFFICE (SCOTLAND),
EDINBURGH, 12*th October* 1932.

CIRCULAR $\frac{G.M.}{243}$

Suspension of Passenger Train Service on Cruden Bay Branch.

The Staff are hereby informed that the Passenger Train Service at the undernoted Stations will be withdrawn during the winter months, as from Monday, 31st October, 1932.

Auchmacoy	Cruden Bay
Pitlurg	Bullers o' Buchan (Halt)
Hatton	Longhaven
Boddam	

Detailed instructions relating to Parcels and Goods Traffic will be issued in due course by the Officers concerned.

J. CALDER,
General Manager, Scotland.

down platform building as a substitute, and an old coach body was brought in to act as a store.

In 1932 it was decided to suspend the branch passenger services during the winter period, the last train running on 29 October of that year. However, the services were not reinstated the following year; indeed, they were never reinstated, and the only passenger trains to use the line again were a few excursion trains and, during World War II, a few troop trains. But despite the loss of the

scheduled passenger services in 1932, goods trains continued operating until 1947. Between then and the time the last sections of track were lifted in the early 1950s, the line found use as a store for withdrawn and crippled wagons.

Following the withdrawal of the branch passenger services, the trams continued to make daily runs to the station mainly to collect the laundry baskets which were now conveyed in a van attached to the daily goods train, plus coal and other goods as required. As

for passengers, in order to cater for its better-off clientele the LNER provided a twice-daily direct limousine service from Aberdeen station to Cruden Bay. This was registered with the Traffic Commissioners as an express bus service, but the vehicle used by the LNER was certainly not a 'bus. It was a 7 seat Rolls Royce Phantom (registration YR 4998) which the LNER had purchased second-hand for £664. The vehicle operated each season from 1933 until 1939.

Everything changed in September 1939. With war looming, the Cruden Bay Hotel was requisitioned by the Government. The last guests left the hotel on 2 September 1939, the same date as the requisition order was signed, and for the next fortnight the hotel was used as a billet for army officers. The staff were vacated on 19 September and the hotel was largely cleared of furniture – tables and chairs from the coffee room were transferred to the station refreshment rooms at Keith Junction station and thus saw further use, but the majority of the hotel furnishings were put into storage, being removed by rail in three batches between September and December 1939. Some of the furniture was stored in the Palace Hotel at Aberdeen but, unfortunately, that hotel was destroyed by fire in 1941.

The original intention was that Cruden Bay Hotel should be used as a military hospital, and elaborate plans were prepared for new lifts, operating theatres and additional buildings within the grounds. Fortunately, though, casualties were less than had been

The two tramcars at their depot at the hotel, sometime in the 1930s. No.2 (on the left) stands on the turntable; No.1 is coupled to the four-wheeled flat truck. PHOTOGRAPH: COURTESY THE GRAMPIAN TRANSPORT MUSEUM

expected, so the scheme was halted and the hotel was used instead as a training or transit base for various regiments, including the Gordon Highlanders.

The hotel tramway closed *circa* March 1941, its duties (by this time, goods only) being taken over by a lorry. The track and the tramcar trucks were sold for scrap, but the tram bodies were acquired by members of the Simmers family of Hatton for use as summerhouses. The hotel laundry and boiler house remained in railway ownership until March 1942. The golf course and a few ancillary properties also remained in railway ownership, being kept on a care and maintenance basis.

The requisition of the hotel eventually led to several years of protracted negotiations with the government's valuers. The hotel itself was derequisitioned in late 1945, but it was summer 1949 before compensation was

agreed at less than the final sum of £19,696.12.1d which the LNER had originally demanded.

After the handing back of the hotel in 1945 the LNER looked closely at the future of the establishment. It was evident that considerable investment and upgrading would be essential if the hotel were to resume its original purpose and, even if this were to be done, the national economic climate raised doubts as to whether the hotel could be restored to profitability. The LNER proposed to concentrate resources, instead, on a replacement for the Palace Hotel at Aberdeen, although in the event the limited funds were used to upgrade the Station Hotel in Guild Street, Aberdeen, another ex-GNSR establishment.

In view of this scenario, in 1946 the LNER opted to place the hotel, its grounds and ancillary buildings on the market. Various possibilities presented

themselves. The favoured use was as a hospital, but the cost of conversion proved too great for the regional hospital board and they bowed out. Other possibilities which manifested themselves at various times included an Air Training Services training school, a workers rest hospital for the Scottish Co-operative Wholesale Society, a Youth Hostel and a Dr.Barnardo's Home. Even Butlin's was canvassed as to possible use as a holiday camp. All this produced one offer for the unacceptably low sum of £7,000.

State ownership

By the time British Railways came into existence on 1 January 1948 the hotel remained unsold. However, BR continued to maintain the golf course with one professional, one green-keeper and three other staff. But the scenario of a nationalised golf course prevailed only until July 1950 when the course and all other related assets were sold for £15,000 to a John Cormie of Glasgow. The deal was partly financed by Glasgow scrap and demolition contractors, John R.Allan & Sons, on the basis that the hotel would be demolished.

Much of the quality granite was sold for building purposes, most notably for Brotherton House, Johnshaven, built by the Aberdeen-based haulage contractor, Charles Alexander. Some other granite went into the construction of local authority flats at Peterhead. Doors, fittings, flooring and other panelling also found use locally.

The golf course was soon resold to an Aberdeen stockbroker who, with two local businessmen, formed the Cruden Bay

Cruden Bay station – two members of staff pose for the camera during one of the many quiet periods. PHOTOGRAPH: GNSRA COLLECTION

The Cruden Bay Hotel 'bus' – the well-appointed and well-polished Rolls Royce limousine – poses for the camera some time in the 1930s. The location is a bit of a mystery – it does not seem to match anywhere in Aberdeen and it is certainly not Cruden Bay. Perhaps it was a convenient spot somewhere near a Rolls Royce dealer or a coachbuilder? PHOTOGRAPH: GNSRA COLLECTION

Golf Club Ltd. It has since been redeveloped so as to remain one of the finest links courses in Scotland. The present magnificent clubhouse, opened in 1998, now almost exactly occupies the site of the old hotel, but an original GNSR pavilion still survives along with traces of the tramway turntable pit.

Into preservation

After the war tramway enthusiasts paid occasional visits to the village of Hatton to seek out the slowly decaying remains of the old Cruden Bay tramcars, in their guise as elegant and unique summerhouses. One enthusiast, Ian Souter, a railway engineer and native of Aberdeenshire, attempted to interest the Grampian Transport Museum at Alford (which was opened in the late 1970s and moved to its current site a few years later) that the restoration of one of the tramcars would be a worthwhile project. However, it was the City of Aberdeen District Council which achieved the trams' initial rescue in 1987, the intention being to restore one of the cars to its original condition. A Community Programme was set up, based on the project being undertaken as training for the unemployed at workshops at Duthie Park, Aberdeen. Dismantling and reinstatement of the timber elements was put in hand, but time and money ran out. Fortunately, though, the council agreed to transfer the project to the Grampian Transport Museum Trust.

The joinery elements of the tramcars were then largely completed with financial support from the Scottish Museums Council and City of Aberdeen District Council. With the help of Ian Souter, the Trust was able to source a truck of the correct age and type from the Tramways Museum in Zurich, Switzerland. This valuable item was donated to the project free of charge, the import being arranged by the Museum Trust with financial assistance from Aberdeen City Council.

For four years the tramcar was exhibited at the Transport Museum as an ongoing restoration project. Reorganisation of Aberdeen Museums led to the ownership of the partly restored saloon passing to the Transport Museum in 1998. At this stage funding was sought for the completion of the project; among the work which still needed to be tackled were:

• completion of the joinery work
• upholstery and curtains
• steps, dashboards and platform ends
• grates, handrails and headlights
• sand-boxes, anti-gallop bars and braking system
• shortening and fitting new suspension system to the ex-Zurich truck
• electrical gear, trolley arm and dummy controllers
• correcting roof distortion, and fitting waterproof roof membrane
• glazing, internal mirrors and light globes
• painting and sign-writing

It was agreed to restore the tramcar to a condition whereby, although it could not be run, it could be fitted with an appropriate electric motor and completed to operational condition at a later date, without reversing the current restoration.

A bonus came with the discovery of copies of the original 1899 drawings at the National Tramway Museum at Crich in Derbyshire. They included actual size templates for metal work. The historical accuracy of the numerous missing parts to be fabricated could thus be guaranteed. Many other original drawings were subsequently found among a collection donated to the Great North of Scotland Railway Association, and these are now on long-term loan to the Transport Museum Trust.

The work was eventually put out to tender and the contract was awarded to the Heritage Engineering of Glasgow. Shortly afterwards the Heritage Lottery Fund, Pilgrim Trust, Hugh Fraser Foundation and the Mercers Society approved the Transport Museum Trust's grant applications, and work finally commenced in January 2000. Restoration was completed and the tram returned to the museum in late August of that year. The formal hand-over before invited guests took place two months later.

The most controversial aspect of the restoration turned out to be choice of livery. The initial assumption had been that the tram had originally been painted in the GNSR carriage livery of purple lake and off-white, but research and analysis of paint samples indicated that had in fact been green and white with elaborate lining and with the dashboard painted purple lake. It was this livery which was adopted by the Trust for the purposes of the current restoration. The interior fabric material of patterned gold satin was replicated using plain contemporary materials.

The restoration of the tram is a tribute to those local entrepreneurs who, in the late 19th century, promoted an ambitious luxury hotel which incorporated the finest furnishings and most up-to-date technology in a relatively remote location. The hotel's demise was perhaps inevitable, due to the short season and relatively poor transport links, but even so it took the outbreak of war to bring about its closure to the public.

As related in the text, Cruden Bay station building was destroyed by fire on 23 April 1931. Some furniture, presumably retrieved from the burning building, sits incongruously in the station forecourt. PHOTOGRAPH: GNSRA COLLECTION

Cruden Bay station – or what was left of it after the fire of 1931. The surviving building is on the down platform – the old coach body, which had been installed for storage purposes after the fire, can be seen. The wagon in the middle of the picture is standing on the tramway turntable; the tramway itself curves away in front of the station master's house. PHOTOGRAPH: ERIC ASHTON COLLECTION

Author's acknowledgements: I have accumulated much further material on the history of the Cruden Bay Hotel and Tramway that may yet form the basis of a book. Help and information has come from many individuals too numerous to mention, but tribute must be paid to Michael Mitchell, Ian Souter, Bill Brown, Mike Ward of the Grampian Transport Museum at Alford, the Great North of Scotland Railway Association, and the staff of the libraries at Aberdeen, Peterhead and the Scottish Record Office, whose assistance in tracing old newspapers and files has proved invaluable.

The Great North of Scotland Railway Association was formed in 1964 to cater for those interested in the history of the former GNSR, its constituents and successors. For details of the GNSRA contact the Membership Secretary, Craighall Cottage, Guildtown, Perth PH2 6DF (we imagine that an s.a.e. would be appreciated) or log on to the society's website at: www.gnsra.org.uk

After the closure of the tramway the bodies of the two tramcars were privately purchased by the Simmers family (the owners of a large bakery business based at Hatton) for use as summer houses at two of the family's homes. By the time this picture was taken in the 1980s one of the properties was owned by the local doctor at Hatton, across the road from the old Hatton station. PHOTOGRAPH: COURTESY THE GRAMPIAN TRANSPORT MUSEUM

On the Light side - I

Two of Britain's best-loved light railways were within only a little more than twenty crow miles of each other. One of the two was the Kent & East Sussex which survived as an independent until 1948 when it was taken into the BR fold. Part of it has, of course, been preserved. These two pictures are from 'independent' days. The upper one is of 0-6-0ST No.4, a one-time LSWR engine, and a pair of ancient four-wheelers at Tenterden Town station. We reckon the date is probably the 1930s as, by the following decade, 'Terriers' were usually used on the passenger jobs. Just mention of the word 'Terrier' and... The lower picture is of K&ES 'Terrier' No.3 which had been purchased by the company in 1901; not only was it to survive in BR service until 1963, but it was subsequently saved for preservation. Here we see it in the shed yard at Rolvenden in May 1947.
PHOTOGRAPHS: THE TRANSPORT TREASURY (upper); DEREK CLAYTON (lower)

On the Light side - II

The other light railway in Kent was the East Kent Light Railway. Like the K&ES it survived as an independent until 1948 when it was taken over by BR. Furthermore, there is now a preservation society based at Shepherdswell. Our upper picture shows the hefty Kerr Stuart 0-6-0T No.4 and the ex-LSWR Adams Radial Tank No.5 in the shed yard at Shepherdswell. The date is obviously pre-March 1946 as, in that month, the Radial Tank was sold to the Southern Railway for use on the Lyme Regis branch. It later became BR 30583 and, after withdrawal in 1961, was acquired by the Bluebell Railway for preservation. Our lower picture shows 0-6-0 No.6 (an ex SE&CR O class) shunting the stock of a mixed train for Wingham into the somewhat basic passenger station at Shepherdswell in September 1948. The Southern station of the same name is out of view to the right. PHOTOGRAPHS: THE TRANSPORT TREASURY (upper); ERIC ASHTON COLLECTION (lower)

THE COLNE VALLEY & HALSTEAD LINE
A keenly contested closure
Notes by I.C.Coleford

Halstead was the largest community served by the CV&H but, to put that into perspective, in the days when the town still had a railway its population was only around 6,000. Nevertheless, the station, although having only one passenger platform, was an impressively spacious affair, a legacy of its days as the headquarters of the Colne Valley & Halstead Railway Company. The building on the far right is, in fact, the old CV&H offices. The building immediately beyond it (and attached to it) used to be stables – the style of the doors is a give-away. The substantial goods shed on the left confirms that the town generated a respectable amount of freight traffic. Among the railway's regular customers there were Courtauld's Textile Mills and Charles Portway's Tortoise Iron Foundry which gained fame for its stoves, the sales pitch being: 'Tortoise' stoves – slow but sure. Also on view are LNER signals on a concrete post. This picture was taken on 20 May 1961. PHOTOGRAPH: JOHN R.BONSER

The Colne Valley & Halstead Railway extended for 19½ miles between Chappel & Wakes Colne in Essex and Haverhill, just over the border in Suffolk. It was a classic country railway which served a handful of small communities; indeed, the largest town along its entire route was Halstead which, even in the 1950s (the last full decade of the railway's life), had a population of less than 6,000.

The CV&H was completed in stages, and was finally opened throughout in May 1863. Like many small local railways it had been promoted and constructed as an independent concern but, whereas most small local companies had a working agreement with a bigger company and, usually, were soon taken over by the larger, 'working' company, the CV&H remained a completely independent, locomotive-owning concern until the Grouping in 1923, when it was taken into the LNER fold.

A journey on the CV&H line had never been particularly speedy; one or more changes of train were required to reach major centres of population such as Colchester or Cambridge, let alone London. Consequently, when motor coaches started to provide competition in the 1920s many locals found that the road transport offered a somewhat speedier – and often more convenient – mode of travel. Nevertheless, the CV&H

line retained its passenger services until the end of 1961 and some of it remained open for goods traffic until 1965.

The history of the Colne Valley & Halstead Railway Company is fascinating, but it has been well documented elsewhere. Furthermore, the story of how the line fared in LNER days has also had a modest amount of coverage in books and magazines. So we do not intend to go over the same ground

again. Instead, we will look at the line in BR days, paying particular attention to the run-up to the closure. For a line which wasn't exactly the most intensively-used in the land – far from it – the closure was very vigorously opposed. As will be seen in the following pages a wealth of documentation from that period survives and, although much of it makes for sad reading, especially for we enthusiasts who can remember the days when the

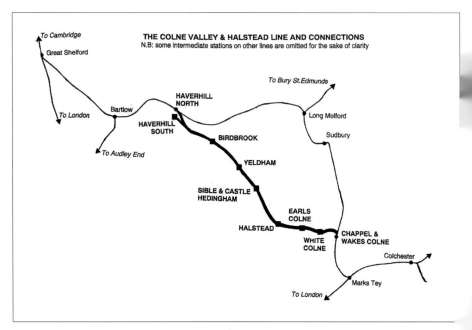

THE COLNE VALLEY & HALSTEAD LINE AND CONNECTIONS
N.B: some intermediate stations on other lines are omitted for the sake of clarity

To Cambridge
Great Shelford
To London
Bartlow
To Audley End
HAVERHILL NORTH
HAVERHILL SOUTH
To Bury St.Edmunds
Long Melford
Sudbury
BIRDBROOK
YELDHAM
SIBLE & CASTLE HEDINGHAM
EARLS COLNE
HALSTEAD
WHITE COLNE
CHAPPEL & WAKES COLNE
Colchester
Marks Tey
To London

CHAPPEL, HALSTEAD AND HAVERHILL NORTH

Single Line
The Haverhill South Single Line connection at Colne Valley Junction is controlled by the Key Token for the Birdbrook and Haverhill North Junction Section.

DOWN — WEEKDAYS / SUNDAYS

M.C.			No. 1	2¼ 3 4 5 6	7 8 9 10 11 12 13 14 15 16	17 18 19 20 21 22
		Description		OP	OP	OP OP	OP	OP
		Class	D		B		

Departs from: Colchester 4.50 a.m. | Mark's Tey 9.26 a.m. | Haverhill N. 11.30 a.m. | Mark's Tey 11.40 a.m. | Haverhill S. 12.40 p.m. | Mark's Tey 6.35 p.m. | Mark's Tey 10 36 a.m. | Mark's Tey 6.28 p.m.

Previous Times on Page: 8 | 8 | 17 | 9 | 17 | 10 | 11 | 11

M. C.			am	am	am am PM	PM PM	PM	am	PM
— —	Chappel		5 45	9 33	11 47	6 43	10 43	6 35
— —	Chappel (S)		5 47	9 34	11 48	4 43 6 46	10 44	6 37
2 10	White Colne			9 38	11 52	4 47 6 51	10 48	6 41
— —	White Colne		✳	9 39	11 53	4 48 6 52	10 49	6 42
3 48	Earls Colne (S) See Note		5 53	9 43	11 56	4 51 6 55	10 53	6 46
— —	Earls Colne (T)		6 3	9 44	11 57	2 32 4 53 6 56	10 54	6 47
6 6	Halstead (T)		6 9	9 49	12 2	2 38 4 58 7 1	10 59	6 52
— —	Halstead		6 40	9 52	12 4	3 10 5 2 7 5	11 3	6 56
9 30	Sible and Castle H. (T)		6 48	9 58	12 10	3 20 5 6 7 11	11 9	7 2
— —	Sible and Castle H.		7 15	10 0	12 12	3 45 5 10 7 13	11 11	7 4
11 72	Yeldham See Note (T)		7 24	10 5	12 17	3 55 5 15 7 18	11 16	7 9
— —	Yeldham		7 50	10 7	12 18	4 25 5 16 7 19	11 18	7 11
15 56	Birdbrook See Note		8 0	10 15	12 25	4 35 5 24 7 26	11 26	7 19
— —	Birdbrook		8 10	10 16	12 26	4 45 5 25 7 27	11 28	7 21
18 31	Colne Valley Junction A				11 39 12 49			
— —	Haverhill South				11 43			
19 41	Haverhill North (T)		8 25	10 24	12 34 12 53	4 57 5 33 7 35	11 36	7 29
— —	Haverhill North				5 15		11 40	7 32

Arrives at: Cambridge 6.14 p.m. | Cambridge 12.17 p.m. | Cambridge 8.10 p.m.

Forward Times on Page: 9 | 11 | 11

Notes:
11 To leave Haverhill, with traffic for Cambridge and via Cambridge only.

Distance from Colne Valley Junction to Haverhill South is 55 chains.

A—Auxiliary Key Token instrument provided for working connection at Haverhill South.

Earls Colne and Yeldham
A passenger train must not cross another passenger train at these stations.

Birdbrook
Electric Token Station but not a crossing place.

HAVERHILL NORTH, HALSTEAD AND CHAPPEL

Single Line
The Haverhill South Single Line connection at Colne Valley Junction is controlled by the Key Token for the Haverhill North Junction and Birdbrook Section.

UP — WEEKDAYS / SUNDAYS

	No. 1	2 3 4 5 6	7 8 9 10 11 12 13¼ 14 15 16	17 18 19 20 21 22
Description		OP	OP	OP OP	OP	OP
Class		B		B		

Departs from: Cambridge 6.28 a.m. | Coldham Lane 6.35 a.m. | Cambridge 8.0 a.m. | Cambridge 3.50 p.m.

Previous Times on Page: 12 | 12 | 15 | 15

M. C.			am	am	am am PM	PM PM PM	am	PM
— —	Haverhill North		7 12	8 5		2 5 3 15 5 58	8 40	4 30
— —	Haverhill North (T)		7 30	8 35	9 20 11 30		8 43	4 37
	Haverhill South				12 40			
— —	Colne Valley Junction A				11 34 12 44			
— —	Colne Valley Junction				11 39 12 49			
3 66	Birdbrook See Note		7 38	8 47	9 28	2 13 3 26 6 6	8 51	4 45
— —	Birdbrook		7 39	9 0	9 29	2 14 3 35 6 7	8 53	4 46
7 50	Yeldham See Note (T)		7 46	9 10	9 36	2 21 3 45 6 14	9 1	4 54
— —	Yeldham		7 48	10 10	9 37	2 22 4 20 6 15	9 3	4 55
10 12	Sible and Castle H. (T)		7 53	10 18	9 42	2 27 4 28 6 20	9 8	5 0
— —	Sible and Castle H.		8 0	11 10	9 44	2 30 5 11 6 22	9 10	5 2
13 36	Halstead (T)		8 6	11 20	9 50	2 36 5 21 6 28	9 16	5 7
— —	Halstead		8 10	1 0	9 58	2 41 6 0 6 30	9 20	5 12
15 74	Earls Colne See Note (T)		8 15	1 8	10 3	2 46 6 35	9 26	5 18
— —	Earls Colne (S)		8 16		10 5	2 48 7 5 6 36	9 30	5 22
17 32	White Colne		8 20		10 9	2 52 6 39	9 31	5 23
— —	White Colne		8 21		10 10	2 53 ✳ 6 40	9 35	5 25
19 41	Chappel (S)		8 25		10 14	2 57 7 18 6 44	9 37	5 28
— —	Chappel		8 27		10 16	7 30 6 49		

Arrives at: Mark's Tey 8.34 a.m. | Mark's Tey 10.23 a.m. | Haverhill South 11.43 a.m. | Haverhill North 12.53 p.m. | Colchester 8.45 p.m. | Mark's Tey 6.56 p.m. SX Colchester 7.12 p.m. SO | Mark's Tey 9.44 a.m. | Mark's Tey 5.35 p.m.

Forward Times on Page: 12 | 12 16 | 16 | 14 | 14 | 15 | 15

Notes:
15 Mark's Tey arr. 6.56 p.m. SX Colchester arr. 7.12 p.m. SO

Distance from Haverhill South to Colne Valley Junction is 55 chains.

A—Auxiliary Key Token instrument provided for working connection from Haverhill South.

Birdbrook
Electric Token Station but not a crossing place.

Yeldham and Earls Colne.
A passenger train must not cross another passenger train at these stations.

Working timetable 27 September 1948 until further notice.

---

railway map of Britain had an almost full set of rural branch lines, it provides an insight into what went on at times like this.

..........ooooo00ooooo..........

By the start of the BR era in 1948 the Colne Valley & Halstead line was served by just four passenger trains each way on weekdays and one on Sundays. Come summer the line also saw a Cambridge-Clacton through train; this was a long-standing 'Summer Only' working which included through coaches for Walton-on-Naze.

Another feature of operations was the provision of through coaches from the Colne Valley Line to Colchester. For example, the 2.19pm ex-Haverhill was attached at Chappel to the 1.24pm (1.33pm on Saturdays) Cambridge-Colchester train. The coaches returned from Colchester at 4.13pm, being detached at Chappel at 4.35pm.

In those days the usual motive power for the passenger trains was a mix of J15 0-6-0s and E4 2-4-0s, while the goods workings were invariably handled by the J15s. So to outward appearances the

In the days when the CV&H was an independent concern its trains started and terminated at Chappel & Wakes Colne station, but in LNER and the BR steam era some of the trains ran through to/from Marks Tey. This is J15 65465 waiting at the branch platform at Marks Tey with the 12.01pm Colne Valley Line train on 16 October 1954. Although this picture (and all of the others which include locomotives) show smokebox-first running, five of the twelve workings on the Colne Valley Line involved tender-first running. Although there was a turntable at Marks Tey, it was only 46ft 6in diameter which meant that the larger engines could not use it. PHOTOGRAPH: PHILIP J.KELLEY

Colne Valley Line seemed like a typical ex-Great Eastern country branch line; the only flaw was that it had never been part of the Great Eastern!

However, the GE influence was soon diluted as, during June and July 1951, some of the passenger workings were taken over by Ivatt Class 2 2-6-0s from Colchester and Cambridge sheds. A

visitor to the line in early 1952 reported that '...traffic is quite encouraging, although prospects for the adjoining Cambridge-Sudbury line are poor'. A return visit on 20 December 1952 found

Manoeuvring at Marks Tey on 19 February 1949. J15 65473 of Colchester shed is positioning coaches in the branch platform. In front of the engine are coaches and an interesting old van for Sudbury while behind it are ancient-looking coaches for the Colne Valley Line. PHOTOGRAPH: JOHN MEREDITH

ESTIMATED SAVINGS FROM WITHDRAWAL OF PASSENGER SERVICE
BETWEEN HAVERHILL AND CHAPPEL AND WAKES COLNE VIA HALSTEAD
AND COMPLETE CLOSURE OF LINE BETWEEN COLNE VALLEY JUNCTION
(EXCLUSIVE) AND YELDHAM (EXCLUSIVE)

	Per Annum	
	£	£
(A) IMMEDIATE AND SHORT TERM SAVINGS OF WORKING EXPENSES		
(1) Staff costs	12,888	
(2) Repair of rolling stock	1,458	
(3) Train movement costs, other than staff	776	
(4) Day-to-Day costs in the repair of permanent way, bridges, buildings, signalling, roads, fences, etc., and day-to-day costs of working stations and signals, other than staff.	1,230	
	16,352	
(B) PROVISIONS FOR RENEWAL SAVED.		
(5) Rolling stock and plant	950	17,302
DEDUCT:		
(C) ESTIMATED LOSS OF GROSS RECEIPTS		
(6) Passenger	5,550	
(7) Freight	1,610	
(8) Miscellaneous	100	
	7,260	
(D) ESTIMATED COST OF PROVIDING ALTERNATIVE ROAD SERVICES IN LIEU OF RAIL SERVICES	120	7,380
(E) NET ESTIMATED SAVINGS FROM CLOSING OF BRANCH		
(A + B - C - D) before including any savings in connection with renewal of permanent way, signalling, structures, etc.		9,922

(F) THE NET ESTIMATED SAVINGS AT (E) DO NOT INCLUDE ANY
PORTION OF THE UNDERNOTED RENEWALS EXPECTED TO BE
REQUIRED IN THE FIVE YEARS ENDING IN 1965

	Permanent way, signalling, bridges, buildings, roads, fencing etc.
	£
in year 1961	17,350
in year 1962	8,200
in years 1963 to 1965	1,850
Total during five years ending in 1965	27,400

Line Traffic Manager (Great Eastern)
Eastern Region,
British Transport Commission.

EE/47/9

2nd December, 1960.

Colchester's 46469 on the 11.59am Marks Tey-Haverhill which consisted of two modern semi-corridor coaches. Arrival at Haverhill, at 12.52pm, was nine minutes ahead of the Marks Tey-Long Melford-Cambridge train which provided a connection from the Colne Valley Line to Cambridge. Our visitor also noted J15 65445 shunting at Halstead goods yard and another Colchester Ivatt, 46468, at Haverhill.

In the summer of 1954 the provision of through coaches to/from Colchester was withdrawn.

Although the Ivatt Class 2s performed very well on the line, the J15s made something of a comeback. Indeed, a visit to the line on 8 September 1956 found 65438 waiting at Marks Tey with the 11.57am to Haverhill whilst 65445 was waiting to follow on with a goods. A third

J15, 65467 of Ipswich, was shunting at Haverhill. However, the Ivatts later returned to the line and it fell to one of the class to perform the last scheduled steam working on Saturday 27 September 1958. The following day diesel railbuses took over, though the goods workings were subsequently handled by J15s and, later, diesels (mainly BTH 'Type 1s').

Despite the introduction of railbuses on the ordinary workings, steam continued to appear on excursion and special workings. Among these were the traditional Halstead Co-operative society annual excursions to the coast. The last steam-hauled excursion on the Colne Valley Line operated during the summer of 1961. As far as we are aware the very last known special passenger working on the line was diesel-hauled.

This was the 'Colne Valley Ramblers' special of Sunday 8 October 1961 which, with BTH 'Type 1' D8236 in charge, started at Liverpool Street and ran via Bartlow and Haverhill where it picked up the Colne Valley Line and ran through to Marks Tey. Accounts of the trip indicate that the train conveyed a number of railway enthusiasts as there are reports of it stopping at each the stations on the Colne Valley Line for photographic purposes.

Going back to the everyday matters of 1959, the regular users of the railway hoped that the introduction of railbuses would bring about an improvement in the frequency of services, but although there were improvements they were minimal. In the Up direction, an additional early morning Halstead-Marks Tey local was provided as from 5 January 1959; this was worked by the 6.35am Cambridge-Marks Tey railbus which returned light to Halstead for an 8.39am departure. The idea behind this extra working was that it offered a good connection with a London train at Marks Tey but the service was poorly patronised – it carried an average of just six passengers each day – and was taken off in November.

Those who hoped that there would be additional services received another blow as the ordinary year-round Sunday services were withdrawn. The only Sunday workings that remained were the 'Summer Only' Cambridge-Clacton through trains; these often comprised eight coaches – a very hefty train for such a little railway – and continued to be steam-hauled, usually by Ivatt Class 2s.

One thing which hampered the Colne Valley Line was that the connections weren't always very useful. For example, anyone wishing to travel on the first Up train of the day from a station on the Colne Valley Line to London was faced with a thirty minute wait at Marks Tey for the London train. In some cases, through journeys between the Colne Valley Line and London required two changes – one at Marks Tey and another at Chappel & Wakes Colne. That said, by the 1950s passengers in the Colne Valley Line's catchment area who needed to travel by rail to or from London – or, for that matter, any other distant destination – had long since got into the habit of being taken to the nearest main line station and getting a fast train from there.

Despite the introduction of the railbuses – i.e. modernisation – in 1958, rumours about the possible closure of the Colne Valley Line had already started to circulate. However, it was the summer of 1960 before it was formally announced that there would be an investigation 'with a view to the line's closure'. Almost all closure threats of the period (and remember that this was pre-Beeching) met with a degree of local opposition but, even so, the protests over the potential closure of the Colne Valley Line were exceptionally loud and long. Matters went as far as a public enquiry, which was held at Halstead Co-operative Meeting Hall in February 1961, and the TUCC, which normally went into 'rubber

Above. E4 62786 crosses over from the main line to the branch platform at Marks Tey on 9 October 1951. We suspect that this is a Stour Valley Line working, but what the heck – it is a lovely picture and shows Marks Tey which, after all, is pertinent to the story. That's our argument, M'Lud, and we're sticking to it. PHOTOGRAPH: DEREK CLAYTON

stamp' mode, showed uncharacteristic resilience and recommended that the line should remain open for a further twelve months. Somewhat ironically, on one of the few occasions the TUCC showed some teeth it was over-ruled by the Central Transport Consultative Committee which preferred the withdrawal of passenger services 'sooner rather than later'.

The withdrawal of passenger services was set for Monday 1 January 1962. In the absence of Sunday services the last scheduled trains ran the previous Saturday, 30 December. The very last working – a DMU – left Marks Tey at 7.06pm with a couple of dozen locals and a similar number of enthusiasts on board. On arrival at Halstead there were the seemingly obligatory detonators, but otherwise there was comparatively little in the way of a send-off, even at the end of the journey at Haverhill.

Despite the withdrawal of passenger services, only the section northwards from Yeldham closed completely. The other parts of the line remained open to goods traffic; Haverhill South itself remained open, and continued to be served from Haverhill North while, to the south, the section between Chappel and Yeldham remained open, being served from the Chappel end. The Chappel-Yeldham section was served by a train each morning, the usual motive power being a 'Type 1' BTH diesel (D82XX).

(ii) Particulars of train services to be withdrawn including number of trains per day and average interval.

	Winter ~ 12/9/60		Summer 1960	
	Weekdays		Weekdays	Suns.
First and Last Trains	U 7.24am ex Haverhill D 8.21am ex Marks Tey D 10. 8am ex Chappel U 6.13pm ex Haverhill D 7. 6pm ex Marks Tey		U 7.24am ex Haverhill D 8.21am ex Marks Tey D 10. 8am(10. 4am SO) ex Chappel. U 6.15pm ex Haverhill. D 7.17pm(7.06pm SO) ex Marks Tey.	U 8.35am ex Haverhill. D. 6.25pm ex Marks Tey.

Trains per day		M/F	Sat.	Average interval M/F	Average interval Sat.	M/F	Sat.	Sun.	Average interval M/F	Average interval Sat.	Sun.
				Mins.	Mins.				Mins.	Mins.	Mins.
x Chappel & Wakes Colne	U	4	5	216	162	5	5	1	162	162	–
	D	4	4	181	181	4	4	1	188	183	–
White Colne	U	3	4	274	182	3	3	–	187	187	–
	D	3	3	203	203	4	3	–	188	217	–
Earls Colne	U	4	5	216	162	5	5	1	162	162	–
	D	4	4	181	181	4	4	1	188	182	–
Halstead	U	4	5	216	162	5	5	1	162	162	–
	D	5	6	162	130	5	6	1	168	130	–
Sible & C.H.	U	4	5	216	162	5	5	1	162	162	–
	D	4	5	181	136	4	5	1	188	137	–
Yeldham	U	4	5	216	162	5	5	1	162	162	–
	D	4	5	181	136	4	5	1	188	137	–
Birdbrook	U	4	5	216	162	5	5	1	162	162	–
	D	4	5	181	136	4	5	1	188	137	–
x Haverhill	U	4	5	216	162	5	5	1	162	162	–
	D	5	6	163	130	5	6	1	168	130	–

D = Down Trains.   SO = Saturdays Only.
U = Up Trains.   x = Colne Valley Line Trains Only.
M/F = Mons. to Fris.

(iii) Average number of passengers joining and alighting at each station per day.
(a)

	Mon. to Fri.				Saturdays x				Sunday x			
	Week-ended				Week-ended				Week-ended			
	27.2.60		20.8.60		27.2.60		20.8.60		27.2.60		20.8.60	
	J.	A.	J.	A.	J.	A.	J.	A.	J.	A.	J.	A.
✗ Chappel & W.C.	22	15	60	56	27	9	8	9				1
White Colne	2	1	4	4	1	1	8					
Earls Colne	4	3	8	10	13	11	4	9				
Halstead	25	24	49	53	67	66	102	86	N. S.		18	16
Sible & Castle												
Hedingham	31	36	30	28	26	37	42	23			14	10
Yeldham	23	20	20	21	40	25	54	25			15	15
Birdbrook	3	3	3	4	11	10	7	9			1	2
✗ Haverhill	34	30	44	29	52	32	67	39			12	19

A = Alighting.   N.S. = No Service.
J = Joining.   x = Actual Number.
✗ = Colne Valley Line Passengers Only.

But that situation did not prevail for too long as at the end of 1964 the southern section was truncated at Halstead. The remaining section of the line (Chappel & Wakes Colne-Halstead) closed completely in April 1965. The last goods working had been on 15 April (Maundy Thursday) 1965; it had left Halstead at 3.30pm, the diesel locomotive having two vans and some empty coal trucks in tow.

Contributor's note: During the preparation of these notes reference was made to The Colne Valley and Halstead Railway *by R.A.Whitehead & F.D.Simpson (Oakwood Press 1988), From* Construction to Destruction *by Edward P.Willingham (Halstead & District Local History Society 1989) and various contemporary magazines especially the* Railway Observer. *Thanks are due to Mr.Bryan L.Wilson for advice and assistance.*

Right.. Railbuses were introduced on the Colne Valley Line in 1958. In some quarters there were hopes that BR would make the most of the vehicles and drastically improve the level of services on the line, but that didn't happen. If anything, the unreliability of the railbuses caused the level of service to deteriorate. Here, German-built railbus E79961 waits at the branch platform at Marks Tey. It has arrived with the 11.50am ex-Haverhill and, despite what it says on the blind, its next job will be either back to Haverhill via the Colne Valley Line or to Cambridge via the Stour Valley Line. PHOTOGRAPH: JOHN R.BONSER

Below. Colne Valley trains working through to or from Marks Tey had to cross the magnificent viaduct at the south end of Chappel & Wakes Colne station. The viaduct was – nay, still is – the largest in Essex; it has 32 arches each of 35ft span, is 355ft long and 75ft high. It cost £32,000 to build (a whopping sum in 1849), and over 7,000,000 bricks were used in its construction. Now... having amazed you with those facts and figures, we ask you to bear in mind that the viaduct was *not* on the old Colne Valley & Halstead line itself. Although used by some trains off the Colne Valley Line, the viaduct was on the old Colchester, Stour Valley & Halstead Railway – the 'Stour Valley' line – which became part of the GER. This picture was taken on 27 November 1954. PHOTOGRAPH: PHILIP J.KELLEY

COLNE VALLEY LINE.

SUMMARY OF OBJECTIONS.

RT. HON. R. A. BUTLER, M.P.
STANSTEAD HALL, HALSTEAD, ESSEX. (1st submission dated 8.10.60)

As the Parliamentary Representation for the area, I am naturally most concerned at the proposal to close the Colne Valley Railway Line, and I wish to emphasize the representations I have already made to the Chairman of the B.T.C.

We do not want Halstead to be cut off from passenger train contact with the world outside. It is felt that a modern approach, with a realistic and up-to-date service, will bring back the passengers, whose present lack because of the poor service, is the main justification for the proposal to close the line.

Electrification of the line to Witham, and perhaps to Colchester, seems to me to give B.T.C. an excellent opportunity to provide the kind of service which will command the support of increasing numbers of passengers. I am convinced that there is nothing in the present situation which cannot be overcome by improved services. Further, I do not understand why Halstead should suffer with a poor rail service, or perhaps none at all, as compared with the nearby similar town of Sudbury, which seems to be well served.

(2nd submission dated 9.12.60)

I have already made official representations to the Transport Users Consultative Committee in my capacity as M.P. against the closure of the Colne Valley line to passenger service.

I now write as a local resident to make a further plea for the improvement of the passenger service. I am more than ever impressed by the very serious car parking difficulties at all the local main line stations. Many residents here travel daily to and from London and the need for a train service to suit business people in the Colne Valley is of increasing importance.

It is my firm consideration that a service has never been provided really to suit the needs of local residents. I have represented the district for 31 years and I feel very deeply that we are being, and have been, let down by the B.R.(E).

MR. P. J. CUTLER, M.A., 77 KING'S ROAD, HALSTEAD.

During 1959, a diesel car used to leave Halstead for Marks Tey at about 8.40 a.m., providing a speedy and excellent connection with a London bound express. I travelled several times by this train, and found it not only efficient but — more important — well patronised. Then, towards the end of the year, it was abruptly withdrawn. The booking staff of Halstead station — among others — expressed amazement, as they were convinced that this excellent service had paid for itself. This was denied by a B.R. representative at a public meeting held in Halstead last September. He may have been right: he no doubt had access to the statement of returns, but it is certain that this train came much nearer to paying for itself than many a service on the C.V.R. in recent years. The sensible course, surely, would have been to implement this service in some way, at least as an experimental measure, to see if it would fulfil the definite promise which it showed. Instead of this, it was deleted, and we were left with services such as I detailed in my earlier letter. Where, Sir, is the sense of this ?

MR. E. B. THORP, 258 ELM ROAD, LEIGH-ON-SEA, ESSEX. (5.12.60)

I write to strongly protest against the proposal to withdraw the passenger service on the Colne Valley Railway. Although I do not reside in the Halstead area, I spend most weekends either in Halstead or Haverhill and always avail myself of the passenger train facilities, both for the purpose of getting from one place to another and to enjoy the scenic amenities of this pleasant line.

I feel no effort has been made to attract passenger business. For example from Haverhill to Chappel via Halstead there is no train from 9.30 a.m. until 3.20 p.m., a gap of six hours without a train. This situation you will agree is quite preposterous.

No person can say that such a service is adequate. "Would be" passengers cannot travel in "non existent" trains, and new business will not be gained.

The line should be given a chance to work. I can tell you from experience the staff of this line are exceptionally helpful, polite and conscientious — very different from some on the Southend-Fenchurch Street line, which I also use. You have on the one hand this excellent staff throughout the sector, yet on the other hand, no trains for long periods during the day. How discouraging and unfair for the staff to have to tell would be passengers to travel by bus, as there is no train for literally hours. The staff must feel this is a "Cinderella" Line. As for modernisation, they are not even given a pot of paint, and how a pot of paint can work wonders!!

If this proposal to withdraw passenger services was put into force, more travellers would be forced to use the already over congested roads. The bus services are poor, very slow and uncomfortable.

Also I think it must be borne in mind that if passenger facilities are withdrawn on the Colne Valley Railway, and even if you assure firms of continuing goods facilities, these same firms will see the red light, and gradually transfer to lorries, rather than be left high and dry at a later date should it be decided to close the line entirely.

In any case the passenger service of the Colne Valley Railway should be looked upon as a public amenity. The railway will be in use for goods transport, so the passenger service should be retained. The G.P.O. do not close letter boxes throughout the country, because there are few letters in them. The Postmaster General has said the amenity must be available to all, even if unremunerative at times.

However, with regard to the finances of the matter on the Colne Valley Railway, no effort seems to have been made to run an economic service. The rolling stock is varied, some diesel railcars, some diesel twin sets — a steam train, the latter with dirty carriages, torn upholstery, unclean windows, etc., sometimes four carriages long when two would suffice. There seems no responsible man at the "head of things". Why has a trial period of railcars not been tried ? (with improved frequency of course). This innovation would give the line a chance to compete, to attract business and serve as an encouragement to the staff. They must surely feel this year that a deliberate attempt has been made to lose custom and so say the line does not pay.

Chappel & Wakes Colne station, 22 August 1959. The Colne Valley Line diverged from the Stour Valley line just beyond the road bridge in the distance. Colne Valley passenger trains used both platforms. The station is still in use today, being served by Marks Tey-Sudbury trains; nowadays there are sixteen Down and eighteen Up trains on weekdays and fourteen each way on Sundays – a far, far better level of services than there ever was in the 'old days'. But although the station is well-served, it now has only one platform – the down platform (on the left). Now, the station building and the goods shed and yard are occupied by the East Anglian Railway Museum. PHOTOGRAPH: JOHN R. BONSER

WHITLOCK BROS.LIMITED, GREAT YELDHAM, ESSEX.

As perhaps one of the largest users of facilities on the above line, we wish to register in the strongest possible terms, our objection to the T.U.C.C.'s proposal to withdraw the passenger service on this line and to the closure of the line from Yeldham to Haverhill.

1. The cost of Rail charges to us on our traffic, which has been increasing year by year, amounts to something between £7,000 and £10,000 per annum, of which approximately one third is for passenger traffic. We estimate that our existing traffic may well be doubled in the foreseeable future.

2. None of our 600 work people use passenger trains from the Halstead direction because the services are inadequate and in no way related to normal working hours.

3. At the moment we are able to despatch urgent spares from Yeldham Station either to the London area (five services per day) or to the Cambridge area (five services per day). This means that goods for which we receive orders in the morning post can be delivered to the station immediately and reach London by mid-day, which ensures that machines are put back into work immediately. The very nature of our machines is such that supplies of spare parts must be immediately available, gang labour being attached to work behind them - consequently the machines must be kept constantly at work.

4. *Export.* At the moment many urgent spares orders received from overseas are received by cable overnight and are sent by passenger train to Liverpool Street Station first thing next morning from where they are collected by our London agents and transferred to the airport. This means they arrive overseas 24 hours earlier than would be the case if the present service is dispensed with.

5. *Collections.* It appears there will only be one collection of passenger traffic per day - that is for goods to Cambridge and the Midlands for despatch on the 5.22 p.m. train, and for Colchester and London on the 6.27 train, as against the five deliveries and collections at present in operation at Yeldham.

6. *Delivery of Urgent Parcels.* The closing of the Yeldham - Haverhill section would mean that in future we would have to travel 30 miles by road to Marks Tey, or 16 miles by road to Haverhill to ensure urgent delivery of goods by passenger train.

7. *Steel and Incoming Goods from South Wales and the Midlands.* Deliveries have proved most practicable and efficient travelling via Cambridge and Haverhill to Yeldham. Closure of this section would involve this traffic in considerable additional mileage travelling on from Haverhill to Chappel or Colchester, and then being transhipped back to Great Yeldham. This would mean at least 24 hours delay on all incoming goods from the South Wales or Midlands areas and involve us or the Railways in additional cost. This would most seriously affect our whole production, which is predominately export at the present time. An alternative of course would be for us to have the steel sent Carriage Paid Home to Clare Station and for the Railway Company to deliver it into our Works by road, or alternatively for us to arrange road transport direct from the Steel Mills.

8. *Additional Traffic.* At the moment the Railways are only getting a very small proportion of our traffic and a concerted effort to obtain more of this - and probably the same applies to all other industries in the area - might well put the line on a more economical basis. As a case in point, between one thousand and two thousand tractor units are brought in by road to Great Yeldham from the Ford Motor Company's Works at Dagenham each year and I do not recall the Railway Executive submitting a price to us in an endeavour to secure this business.

Finally, we shall oppose to our utmost any steps being taken to deprive this growing industrial community of its Transport and Passenger facilities feeling that provided certain economies are introduced in the Railways present labour force, the Colne Valley Line can be made to pay its way. One is tempted to enquire whether the Consultative Committee have taken any steps to make approaches to the several industrial firms and manufacturers who have recently established themselves in the Colne Valley at Halstead, Haverhill etc. to ascertain to what extent these firms can offer support, and whether the continual industrial expansion envisaged in the area has been given sufficient thought.

YELDHAM & DISTRICT WOMEN'S INSTITUTE.

With reference to the proposed closing of the Colne Valley Railway; the members of the Yeldham & District Women's Institute would like to object for the following reasons :-

(a) It is impossible to get to Halstead for shopping in the morning and arrive back in time for dinner, or to go shopping in the afternoon and get back in time for tea.

(b) A great many of our members are unable to travel on coaches, owing to travel sickness.

(c) It will be impossible for residents to get to Cambridge.

(d) Mothers will be unable to take their small children shopping because prams cannot be conveyed on buses.

In conclusion, more people from this area would travel to and from London by train if services were more convenient and there were not so many changes.

FRANCIS N. ADAMS (Retired Wine & Spirit Merchant), Nornington House, Colchester Road, HALSTEAD.

As a life long resident of the Colne Valley and with my home in Halstead I have for a very long period enjoyed the convenience of the above Branch Line and I therefore deeply regret that the British Transport Commission are now seriously considering the withdrawal of passenger services from this line. I go further and protest most strongly against any such shortsighted action being taken.

There are many reasons for this protest but perhaps the most important is the industrial development now taking place in the Colne Valley and which is likely to continue with the need of having a railway for all services running through the area.

Then the ordinary passenger has the right to be able to start his journey from his own station or one fairly close at hand instead of having to travel by car or motor bus to join a train, anything from 6 to 20 miles distant. For my own part I like to be able to start from my own station and this is specially convenient when travelling with luggage.

TOPPESFIELD PARISH COUNCIL.

The question of the closure of the Colne Valley passenger service was considered at a recent meeting of this Parish Council, and they wish to make it clear that they have serious objections to this and it is hoped that a representative will be able to attend any meeting in connection with retaining this service. Objections to the closure are listed below :-

1. Mothers with young children cannot get to Halstead for shopping as the buses do not cater for carrying prams.

2. The bus service to Halstead takes far longer than the train.

3. The train service to the coast is much appreciated in the summer, and if people from Gt.Yeldham and Toppesfield have to make their own way to Colchester before they can get to the excursion train it will be much more inconvenient, particularly where families with young children are concerned, and changing buses etc. with tired children rather spoils any enjoyment which may have been had during the day.

4. The diesel train service is a pleasant quick way of getting to Cambridge, via Haverhill; if people have to make their own way to connect at Haverhill it will prove more costly and make a longer journey.

5. Many people appreciate the 'run-about' tickets during their summer holidays, but these will not be able to be taken advantage of if the train service is discontinued.

HALSTEAD & DISTRICT RACING PIGEON CLUB.

On behalf of the above Club I would like to protest against the proposed closure of the Colne Valley Railway.

Our club officials frequently attend London centre meetings, together with visits to Cambridge, Colchester, Chelmsford and Ipswich, in which they always travel by rail.

Railbus E79961 stands at Chappel & Wakes Colne on 27 December 1961; this was three days before the withdrawal of passenger services on the Colne Valley Line. Once again, ignore what it says on the blind; the railbus is waiting at the down platform and will form the 10.08am to Haverhill. PHOTOGRAPH: JOHN R.BONSER

MR. & MRS. A. D. RAYNER and K. RAYNER, 6 THE BUNGALOWS, SIBLE HEDINGHAM, HALSTEAD, ESSEX.

In response to the announcement in the Halstead Gazette, we would like to voice our protest against the closure of the Colne Valley Railway. It is, as you say, the only effective means of "getting out and about" during the summer months and holiday period, as the omnibus services to and from the outlying villages are most inadequate. As we have no car, we are fairly dependent upon the railway (or bus) for any reasonable distance travelled.

Furthermore, my mother is one of those unfortunate people who cannot travel in smelly, grinding, and in many cases, jerky buses, for long distances without feeling ill.

Also, I remember as a schoolboy (not many years ago), having many happy hours with my friends, the engine drivers, who used to break all rules and give me rides on the footplate of the J15s and sometimes, Class 2MTs, and what a thrill it gave me!

We would, indeed, be very sorry to say good-bye to the Colne Valley Railway, but we would like to add one proviso: perhaps if the timetable could be slightly revised to suit the public better, it might mean an increase in passengers carried.

MRS. E. BROWN, 7, HOLMAN ROAD, HALSTEAD, ESSEX.

We the undersigned wish to register our protest in the closing of the Colne Valley Line. This town is very poor now, with a part-time library, a weekly National Insurance Office, bad roads and poor street lighting. We hope the people of this town are awake enough to realise the importance of your splendid appeal.

MR. D. FOSTER, "CHEZ-NOUS", GREENSTEAD GREEN, HALSTEAD, ESSEX.

I wish to register my objection to the closing of the Colne Valley section of B.R. which will in my opinion set back the entire Colne Valley a quarter of a century in relation to progress. This line was pioneered and built by local people and capital and it seems a very poor state of affairs that when it once again belongs to the people of the valley through state ownership, it and those employed on it should be thrown on the scrap heap. The small cost of making good the defective revenue of the line in relation to the vast and flamboyant squandering of the taxpayers hard earned money - and remembering that the residents of the Old Valley are themselves these same taxpayers - is it not better to put employment and public convenience before £100 million worth of useless rockets which will not fly. It is

a small pity that some of the deadwood in the present Government cannot be disposed of as easily as the Colne Valley Railway. This line holds together the local countryside and one has only to stand beside the Colchester - Marks Tey road any summer weekend to realise it is more railways and not less that are needed.

MR. L. D. DARRELL, THE HOWE, HALSTEAD, ESSEX.

I am writing to register my protest and that of my family and staff here to the proposal to close the above Railway. Also my wife's family who live at Littleport where her father is the local Vicar - Canon Payne - make frequent usage of this Railway to travel here via Cambridge and Haverhill.

I have often to motor to Chelmsford or Witham for London myself but I know of several people who would like to see this station at Halstead connected to Marks Tey to join the train that leaves Witham at 9.45 a.m. as I would also.

MR. H. K. TANSWELL, FERNDALE, 29 MORLEY ROAD, HALSTEAD, ESSEX.

I feel concerned at the imminent closure of the Colne Valley Railway and feel that this will cause great inconvenience to people and trading in Halstead and neighbouring villages.

I have in the past frequently used the railway but unfortunately the trains are often late and having bought my train ticket to reach my destination at a reasonable time I have had to hire a taxi. On one or two occasions the train has broken down and taxis have been provided at the expense of the railway which no doubt accounts for some of the loss made.

Businessmen Tell of Railway Difficulties

COLNE VALLEY CLOSURE

Improved Services Urged

When the Transport Users' Consultative Committee resumed the hearing of the British Transport Commission's proposal for the withdrawal of the passenger service from the Colne Valley Railway Line at Halstead yesterday, Mr. J. Harvey, of Colchester Borough Council, said that authority felt Colchester was used for shopping, recreation, school, etc., by people from the area and they opposed the proposed closure. At Colchester they had their own bus service, and they found that when they cut services to curtail financial losses, they lost more money.

Mr. E. P. Willingham, secretary of the Haverhill branch N.U.R., said he must emphasise that the service on the line had become worse during the past few years with a resultant loss of passengers. He said it gave railway employees little pleasure to have to give would-be train passengers information as to alternative transport.

The extraordinary position prevailed on the Colne Valley Railway whereby passengers could not buy return tickets because they could not get back to train. He favoured deferment of the closure proposal until the electrification of the main line at Colchester had been completed and that then the Colne Valley Railway line be given a new deal for a trial period of two years.

FACTORY WORKERS

An industrialist, Mr. A. C. Whitlock, of Great Yeldham, said his company was continuously expanding and employed some 600 people. Every day they had to run 12 coaches and buses to bring people to their factory, and they strongly objected to the closure of this line. To-day the total cost of transporting goods and materials in and out of his factory amounted to £100,000 a year. The railway at that moment got less than 10 per cent. of that traffic, yet he had never been approached about it by the railway authorities.

Mr. Whitlock said his firm's chief exports were hydraulic excavators and earth-moving machinery and that business depended largely on a good spares service. At present they could get these spares to many parts of Europe within a few hours. He was seriously concerned that with the withdrawal of the passenger service and suggested freight traffic changes, his firm would not be able to maintain that service.

"MISLEADING"

The objection of the Halstead and District Chamber of Trade was put by its honorary secretary, Mr. Stephen L. "T" Crawford, who said the Chamber decided that the proposals must be firmly opposed. It was submitted that the Commission's memorandum was misleading and failed to give a true picture either of the present position or of the real intentions.

"Even the heading misleads," said Mr. Crawford, "by referring to 'proposed withdrawal of passenger services and closure of Birdbrook station' whereas the intention is to remove completely the line from Yeldham through Birdbrook to a point called 'Colne Valley Junction' just short of Haverhill station."

What are euphemistically termed "rationalisation proposals" for this

area" amounted to proposals for denuding almost an entire Parliamentary constituency of passenger rail services. The Colne Valley line would become a dead-end goods track from Chappel to Yeldham, with Halstead and the greater part of the Colne Valley deprived of any effective public transport to Haverhill and Cambridge, to Colchester and the East Coast, to Witham, Chelmsford and London. Mr. Crawford said the validity of the Committee's procedure was open to doubt and actual or potential rail users were effectively being denied proper rights of objection.

SERVICE CUT

He said a public meeting called by the Chamber of Trade in September had passed unanimously a resolution expressing concern at the declared intention to withdraw passenger services and called on British Railways to institute a good services of trains with which the line could quickly justify itself. Even Mr. Suddaby had said he was impressed by the interest the meeting raised locally.

The Chamber of Trade submitted that the remedy for the present railway losses laid not in cutting down the size of the system, but rather in improving its efficiency. That was particularly so of the Colne Valley line on which the passenger service was now worse than it was in the 19th century, and had degenerated to such a low level as to be virtually unusable.

Dealing with the B.T.C. statistics, Mr. Crawford said these were based on 1960, a season with the heaviest and most prolonged rainfall on record, which must obviously have had a considerable effect on the numbers travelling, particularly to the coast.

NO EXCURSION

There was a still further deterioration in the services, to the extent that all interested in the matter came to the almost inevitable conclusion that the rail services were made so poor that statistics could be made available to bolster up a case for closing the line. As an example the only Sunday passenger service in the Summer season was the 8.35 ex-Haverhill, which was too early for young children wishing to visit the sea. On Whit-Monday the previous year when this excursion ran an hour later, 270 passengers joined the train at Halstead. On the warmer summer Whit-Sunday there was no seaside excursion on the Colne Valley line.

Regarding the service to and from London, it was not surprise he said Mr. Crawford many the public had drifted away from using the trains for the journey of about fifty miles took more than two hours, with up to three changes, and waiting time of up to forty minutes.

DIESEL TRAINS

The existing rail services from Witham and Chelmsford were already overloaded. It was difficult or impossible to get a seat to Liverpool Street. "Must we be condemned to perpetual standing," asked Mr. Crawford.

The B.T.C. had a duty under the Transport Acts to provide efficient and economic railway services, and there appeared to be no requirement that each and every section should be profit earning.

The Chamber of Trade proposed that there be a detailed examination of the problems in the light of the foregoing remarks and made a number of suggestions for one, two and four-car diesel trains from St. Botolph's, Colchester through to Cambridge, emphasising that St. Botolph's was nearer to the shopping centre than is North Station.

After hearing several more objectors, the Committee completed its hearing. The chairman said they hoped to be able to present their recommendations for the future of the line in the first or second week of next month.

Cutting from the *East Anglain Daily Times* of 22 February 1961.

Another view of Chappel & Wakes Colne station, this time on 22 August 1959. We're beginning to think that the crews in this part of the world were running a 'confuse the passenger' competition as the Cravens DMU at the Up platform, despite showing Sudbury on the blind, is on a Sudbury-Marks Tey-Colchester working. PHOTOGRAPH: JOHN R.BONSER

The northern approach to Chappel & Wakes Colne station – side-window cab E4 62784 approaches with the 11.05am Cambridge-Colchester stopper on 27 November 1954. Once again we are aware that this is not a *bona fide* Colne Valley train, but this is a rather nice picture and we are in the right area. So there. PHOTOGRAPH: PHILIP J.KELLEY

The first station along the CV&H 'proper' was White Colne. Originally titled Colne, it opened with this section of the line on 16 April 1860. It closed in May 1889 but reopened in April 1908, this time as White Colne. Even as late as the 1950s the village it served had a population of just 370. Here we are looking towards Halstead on 27 December 1961. The old coach body – it was an ancient 4 wheeler – served as the waiting room while the goods van body was a lock-up. There was a small goods yard on the far side of the level crossing, but that had no goods shed, only another van body. PHOTOGRAPH: JOHN R.BONSER

SECRETARY'S MEMORANDUM.

THE COLNE VALLEY LINE.

The following notes may help members when considering the recommendation of the East Anglian Area T.U.C.C. that a decision on proposed withdrawal of the passenger train service on the Colne Valley Line, and the proposed severance of the line between Yeldham and Haverhill be deferred until such time as the main line between London and Colchester has been electrified.

The Colne Valley & Halstead Railway was a separate company until 1921, though it was worked by the G.E.R. until it was absorbed into the London and North Eastern Railway. It is a single line linking the towns of Haverhill and Halstead, and connects with the old Great Eastern Line at Chappel Junction. This line, known as the Stour Valley line, also runs to Haverhill via Sudbury and Long Melford. From Haverhill, the line continues on to Cambridge so that both the Stour Valley and the Colne Valley Line are connected with that town.

The Colne Valley Line has been superficially neglected, but is not in a dangerous condition. According to the Heads of Information, £27,400 is needed for renewals in the five years ending 1965, of which £17,350 is scheduled for 1961. But it appears from the evidence of the regional engineer (page 8 (Pink)) that this is part of the normal renewal programme based on the assumption that the line would be retained for passenger traffic indefinitely. Much less would have to be spent if the line is to be continued, as recommended by the Area Committee on a short-term basis only, or if it is to be used for freight only, as is intended by the Region.

Ever since 1918, which is the first year of which records are still available, there have only been four or five trains daily each way on this line, and when buses began to develop in the early 1930's they gradually took the bulk of the local traffic, especially into Colchester, the natural shopping centre.

• •

+ The following figures serve to show the falling off of traffic over the years. The figures relate to all stations on the Colne Valley Line except the junctions at either end - (Haverhill and Chappel).

Year	Passengers.
1938	39,975
1948	32,856
1958	26,368
1960	20,166

The London train connections have always been so bad that they are hardly used at all, and many people go by car or bus from Halstead to Chelmsford, twenty miles away, in order to get a reasonable business service to London.

In 1960, an experimental morning business train was run from Halstead, (pop.6,000) to Marks Tey, to connect with a fast train to London; consequently the journey took 1¼ hours instead of 2 hrs. 9 mins., but the local demand was so poor that after ten months the train was taken off. Objectors say that they had hardly realised that this new train had been put on before it had been taken off again, but it is a fact that in the best month of its operation, August 1960, an average of only ten tickets a day were issued from Halstead to London by all trains.

The Eastern Region state (vide para. 2 of their memo. of 29th November 1960) that "during the last two years diesel unit services have been introduced on this line with the object of improving net revenue by reducing movement costs and stimulating new traffic". They then say "while costs have been reduced, there has been no substantial increase in receipts, and the services remain uneconomic".

It is not necessary to probe very far to find the reason for this seemingly disappointing result. It is obvious that the steps taken to improve the services did not go far enough. Diesel trains replaced steam trains, but they continued to run on the same timings as the steam trains (in some cases involving an even greater number of changes). No attempt was made to run an interval service, or to pick up and set down passengers at whistle stop halts, or to consider the passengers' convenience in any way at all.

The objectors rightly claim that there has always been a totally inadequate and unimaginative schedule on this line. The diesel trains may have achieved a saving in operating costs, but much more was required to secure an increase in revenue. Diesel trains running on a regular interval service, or at least at times suited to the public demand, between the places the public wanted to visit (e.g. Colchester, St. Botolphs) might have stimulated new traffic, and indeed recaptured some of that which had been lost.

The Eastern Region claim that they have tried, but failed, is therefore not very impressive, since the effort was entirely superficial, and showed no real urge to exploit all the latent advantages of modernisation. But even if they had, the one useful experiment of the fast train from Halstead to London indicates that it may be too late to revive this railway, whatever may be done.

The case is unusual inasmuch as the service has been so bad for so long that for once there is no allegation of hardship if the service comes off - not even to schoolchildren. The bulk of objectors complain that if only a proper train service could be run it would be used. Some objectors contend that it has been deliberately run down so that it could be closed, but this is obviously untrue, as it has been operated like this for at least thirty years. In one case, there are 600 work-people at a factory at Great Yeldham adjoining the station, but none of them use the railway as the train service is so bad.

Although the proposed withdrawal has led to great indignation among the inhabitents of the Colne Valley, the Region say that they had not had any substantial requests for improvement in the past, presumably because potential demand had ceased.

A great volume of written objections covering 105 pages of closely typed foolscap has been extracted from the minutes before sending them to members. They are summarised below.

The most important objections have however, been left with the minutes so that members can read them. The objectors are headed by Mr. R.A. Butler, the Home Secretary and Member for Saffron Walden for 31 years. He, like the majority, is convinced that if there is a usefully timed train service it would be used, and feels that his constituents have been let down by British Railways. He feels that a modern approach with a realistic and up-to-date service would bring back the passengers.

Other important objectors are the Essex and West Suffolk County Councils, the Halstead Urban and Rural District Councils, and Whitlock Bros. Ltd., of Great Yeldham. Sir Leslie Plummer, M.P. for Deptford, also supports the objections in principle. There are other objections from the Colchester Town Council; from two Urban and twentyone Parish Councils; three Chambers of Trade; four Trades Unions other than railway unions, twelve Local Associations; nineteen Limited Companies; three Schools; three Associations of railway enthusiasts (who were admitted as objectors without showing any evidence of user), and one hundred and thirty six individuals, some of whom had made two separate representations. There were also four objections from N.U.R. branches or groups of railwaymen. Incidentally the objection from the three schools mentioned above concerned the loss of facilities for excursions etc., rather than train services for getting children to and from school.

The substance of all these objections is to the effect that the service, which could be a valuable asset, is completely inadequate; that no attempts are made to encourage traffic by competitive fares; that there are no trains into Halstead or Colchester at shopping times; that there should be fixed interval services running right through to St. Botolphs Station in the middle of Colchester, instead of arriving at Colchester North Station, which is 1½ miles from the town centre, after two changes; that without the train there would be no means of getting to Cambridge (this is not so; there are buses, but they take a long time, and involve a change); that the 1960 figures of carryings were deflated by bad weather, and should not have been used in evidence; that no attempt has been made to encourage the demand which exists right through the summer to go to Clacton and other seaside places; that the buses which people have to use instead of the railways are too slow compared with the time the trains could take if they were properly run.

The buses to Colchester which take about fifty minutes to do the journey from Halstead, take about the same time as the train at present, but there is no change, the bus service is frequent, and the bus Station is undoubtedly much nearer the shopping centre than the railway Station.

The N.U.R. objections were based, to a considerable extent, on figures extracted from railway booking office records, and other matters which could only have been acquired from the special access which employees have to their employers' affairs. They also disputed the accuracy of the data provided by the Region in the Heads of Information.

A closer view of the 'waiting room' at White Colne. This picture was taken on 16 October 1954 and the 'building' appears to be in rather better cosmetic condition than in our earlier picture. There is a story about an American visitor to the area who, on seeing the old coach body, wrote home about the 'half-timbered medieval station' at White Colne. Just one other thing... we are intrigued by the baskets – one in the foreground and one resting against the 'building'. If anyone can tell us what they were for (pigeons perhaps) we would be very interested, please.
PHOTOGRAPH: PHILIP J. KELLEY

These particular objections are well answered by the
Divisional Traffic Manager, in his comments on the objections
generally - see pages 4 to 9 of Appendix C (white).

A more ingenious argument, which may have influenced
the Area Committee to feel that there was a potential, if not
an actual need, (see their reasons on page 5 of the Minute)
was made out by the Essex County Council Planning Officer
at the Hearing, see Appendix D, page 7 (pink). He contended
that the movement of population out of London into the Colne
Valley area was intended eventually to account for some
50,000 persons. If there were no rail facilities in this area,
however, he contended that this development might well be diverted
to an area much nearer London, with the additional peak traffic
problems into London which would be entailed if this were done.
It was therefore he argued, in the best long-term interest
of the railways to encourage the overspill from London to go
as far out as possible into rural Essex, by providing better
services there, even if these did not run at a profit.

The railway view of the overspill problem is covered in
Appendix C, page 2 (white). They expect that the population will
increase by 8,000 in the next five years, and possibly more later
on, but they take the view that industries will be moved out with
them, so that only a small number of people will go far afield
to work. They assess the increase of passengers who are likely
to use both bus and train in the next five years at 700, which
would certainly not justify retention of any rail service.
They readily accept the view that the present service of trains
is quite inadequate, and that more trains would attract more
passengers, but they do not consider that the possible future
developments in industry indicate that there will be sufficient
new business to cover the running costs of the additional
services, let alone to support the services already operating.

While there would be an improvement in the through
services from Marks Tey to London when the main line is
electrified, the Region do not expect that this would lead
to any great increase in the demand from people in the Colne
Valley. The management assess the additional traffic from
the Colne Valley at about £1,500 per annum as a result of the
improved electric connections at Marks Tey. This would not
in their view justify any improvement of the Colne Valley
services, or even the retention of the present services.

J. C. CHAMBERS.

CC.1010/1/37
14th June, 1961.

Right. Although it had only one platform, Earls Colne was a passing place. This signal was at the east end of the station just before the line became single again. The signal is the up starter. It is an old CV&H signal but the post would originally have had an attractive finial; presumably it had been doctored by the LNER. This picture was taken on 27 December 1961. PHOTOGRAPH: JOHN R.BONSER

Below. Earls Colne station, looking towards Chappel & Wakes Colne on 22 August 1959. The station had been originally listed in the timetables as Ford Gate but had been renamed Colne in 1889 and Earls Colne in 1905. The village it served had a population of 1,844 in the mid-1950s, but when we say 'served', it should be borne in mind that the station was in the middle of nowhere, about ¾ mile from the village. The station building was quite substantial for what was a fairly small wayside station; it had been constructed in 1903 to replace an earlier building. PHOTOGRAPH: JOHN R.BONSER

HALSTEAD URBAN & RURAL DISTRICT
COUNCILS JOINT COMMITTEE

Attwoods,
Halstead,
Essex.

16th August, 1961.

Dear Rab,

Colne Valley Railway.

On returning last night from two weeks abroad I heard with dismay that the closure of part of the Colne Valley Railway line seems imminent. I have learned from a well informed local resident that preparations are in hand for the immediate dismantling of signalling equipment following the closure of the line, the intended date for which is believed to be 10th September next.

Mr. E.B.Parker has very kindly joined me in Mr. Long's office this morning, there being no time to convene the full Committee representing the Joint Councils. We have before us your note dated 5th August, 1961 enclosing the letter dated 3rd August, 1961 from the Minister of Transport to you. We have also noted correspondence in the Times concerning the early closure of the Westerham-Dunton Green branch line.

Although you write that "I cannot see what more I can do", Mr. Parker and I would strongly press that at least you urge the Minister to suspend any closure of the Colne Valley Railway until the end of the holiday period. This will enable our Joint Committee to attend you at Stanstead Hall if you would kindly so agree and thus suspend the closure operation before the matter has gone past the point of no return.

I am sorry to worry you with this during your holiday but you will appreciate that to delay the matter might prove fatal.

Yours as ever,

Theodore Vaizey

Brigadier J.T. de.H. Vaizey.
Chairman.

P.S.   As you are unlikely to have a copy of
Mr. Marples' letter with you I enclose
one.

The Rt. Hon. R.A. Butler, C.H., M.P.
The Home Office,
Whitehall,
London, S.W.1.

WHITEHALL, LONDON S.W.1

17th October, 1961.

Dear Ernest

You have been personally most kind and helpful about the Colne Valley line and I do not think you could have taken more trouble over it. In particular I appreciated your coming to see me. At the same time I feel I must put on record that your decision to close the line will cause intense regret. I think it is a most unfortunate decision in view of the industries in Halstead and the activity of the district and in addition the fact that we are twelve miles from a main line.

What I should now be grateful if you could do would be to issue a statement saying that the line is not going to be pulled up so that there may be a chance of saner counsels prevailing when the electrification to Colchester is complete. It seems extraordinary that a nationalised industry should show so little initiative and so little fairness to our district as it has done and - what is worse - as it appears to be going to do.

John & R.B.Butler

The Rt. Hon. Ernest Marples, M.P.

Below. Moving along to Halstead, this was how the northern approach to the station – the Trinity Street Crossing end – looked on a sunny 22 August 1959. The signal box was built to a local design and dated to *circa* 1891; it had a 39 lever Saxby & Farmer frame. The signal on the concrete post was in a high position to improve sighting. PHOTOGRAPH: JOHN R.BONSER

THE LABOUR PARTY
SAFFRON WALDEN CONSTITUENCY

President: Lady Plummer   *Vice-President:* Alderman S. S. Wilson, C.J

Prospective Parliamentary Candidate: MICHAEL CORNISH

Chairman: Mr A. Stieber
Vice-Chairmen: Mr D. Weaver
Dr W. A. L. Collier
Treasurer: Mr. P. A. L. Bamberger

Secretary/Agent: Mrs B. ELLIOTT
Studio Cottage, Colchester Road, Halstead, Essex
Telephone: Halstead 2556

1st December 1964

Mr. Tom Fraser, M.P.,
House of Commons,
Westminster,
London S.W.1.

Dear Mr.Fraser,
I am watching with interest the newspaper reports
on policy in connection with British Railways.   I note that you have
would not necessarily keep a railway open if it was proved to be
uneconomical.
This I would agree, but experience in these parts
have shown that a railway can be "run down" to proves losses. To give
only ONE example, which actually happened to this Colne Valley railway
which was closed in 1959, excursions were advertised and cancelled without
notice or explanation, excursions were run and not advertised.
The station and buildings, except offices in connection with freight,
 have been left standing empty, and we could certainly use these buildings
for something useful as it is in the centre of the town. The lines
between Haverhill (junction for Cambridge) have been out and destroyed over
bridges and left in some cases in a dangerous condition, but between
Halstead and Colchester the railway is still used for goods and particularly
coal and we have a big coal depot near the railway.   Now we are to lose
this and all coal and goods will have to be delivered by road from
Colchester.   This road between Halstead and Colchester is narrow and
winding and is always being repaired somewhere or other.   The cost of
providing a new road, maintaining it for big coal lorries, the traffic
jams where the road cannot be widened because of houses etc, and the
danger be increased traffic on the roads, would not be compensated by the
closing of the line.
We have not been given adquate alternative transport,
its too long a journey to London by coach, and in the morning the first
bus to Braintree gets there two minutes after the first train leaves.
My son has had to leave home and live in digs because he has to get to
Romford to work. Its a bit ridiculous in this day and age not to be able
to get Ixxx ihxx 36 miles in two hours.   Visitors to hospitals in Colchester
if they livex in a village just outside Halstead have to be prepared to give
up four hours for an hour's visit.   The other big hospital at Cambridge
ia worse, only two buses to Haverhill in a day, and now the railway is to
 be closed from Haverhill to Cambridge.
I hope you will look carefully into the social
consequences of these closures, and possibly find out what has happned to
places like Halstead and district after being closed for five years.
The closing of the line for freight is a burning issue here, and it will
certainly add to our cost of living if all goods have to come by road.

Yours sincerely,

Secretary/Agent

Ex-Colne Valley signalling at Birdbrook, 30 October 1954. The lattice post – rather unusual in this part of the world – supports Up home and Down starter signals. The lower arm is of GE origin but the upper one seems to be older; the spectacle glass for the upper arm is positioned part-way down the post for better sighting. PHOTOGRAPH: PHILIP J.KELLEY

A quiet time of day (there were several of these) at Halstead, 22 August 1959. The station opened on 16 April 1860 and, apart from the reconstruction of the canopy in 1914, the platform buildings were little altered throughout their 101-year life. PHOTOGRAPH: JOHN R.BONSER

FACTORY LANE WEST

Going back along the line for a short distance, a little beyond the south-east end of Halstead station the railway crossed Parsonage Lane adjacent to its junction with Factory Lane West. This picture was taken on 20 May 1961. The lofty signal box – it was 25ft high and had a frame above rail level – had replaced an older 'box which had been demolished in an accident in 1899. Note the block indicators on the cottage wall. PHOTOGRAPH: JOHN R.BONSER

On 14 July 1924 the LNER diverted Colne Valley passenger services from the ex-CV&H station at Haverhill to the ex-GER premises, Haverhill North. This was the scene at the latter on 7 April 1958 with J15 65441 pulling in with a hefty Colchester-Cambridge (Stour Valley) train. The point where the spur to the ex-CV&H line diverged is out of view in the distance. PHOTOGRAPH: P.B.BOOTH; NEVILLE STEAD COLLECTION

Left. Following the diversion of the Colne Valley passenger services to Haverhill North in 1924 the old CV&H station (Haverhill South) was retained for goods traffic. This was the view from the buffer stops on 20 May 1961 – the old platform is on the left, the goods shed is beyond it and the water tower is on the right. PHOTOGRAPH: JOHN R.BONSER

Below left. Clearly, there was still some goods traffic being dealt with at Haverhill south on 20 May 1961. The line on the extreme left was once inside an engine shed; the shed closed in 1947, having latterly been a sub-shed of Bury St.Edmunds, but it is unclear whether any engines were actually based there or whether the establishment was by that time merely a signing-on point. By the time this picture was taken the water tank seems not to be used – at least, not for railway purposes as there is no apparent means of getting water to a locomotive. PHOTOGRAPH: JOHN R.BONSER

Below. Looking out from the herbaceous Haverhill South, 20 May 1961. The connection to the spur which led to the ex-GER station is almost ¾ mile away in the distance. PHOTOGRAPH: JOHN R.BONSER

Bylines by the sea (or Going for a Paddler)

And finally...

To round off this late-summer volume we head off to the water. We admit that this splendid paddler, the famous P.S.CONSUL, was not railway-owned but it *did* work at Weymouth where there was a long history of railway company shipping so we reckon it is fair game for inclusion here. CONSUL started life in a different guise, having been built as P.S.DUKE OF DEVONSHIRE by R.& H.Green of Blackwall in 1896 for the Devon Steamship Company for leisure service on the south coast from Exmouth and Torquay. Her vital statistics were 175ft in length, 257 g.r.t and a service speed of 13 knots. During World War I she was used by the Admiralty as a minesweeper in the Mediterranean and the Dardanelles but she returned to civilian life in 1920 and in 1932 was sold for service at Cork. In 1936 she returned to South Devon, this time working for Alexander Taylor of Torquay, but in 1938 she was sold to Cosens & Co for service out of Weymouth. For her new role she was renamed P.S.CONSUL. She was extensively rebuilt in 1948 and remained on Cosens' routes at Weymouth until 1962. Our picture shows her in Cosens' service in August 1960. In 1963 she was sold to New Belle Steamers for service on the Thames and Sussex coast but she returned to Weymouth in 1964. A few years later she was sold for use as an accommodation ship at Dartmouth and reverted to her original name. She was scrapped in 1968, having latterly claimed the status of Britain's longest-serving paddle steamer. PHOTOGRAPH: ERIC ASHTON COLLECTION